NO FEAR

OTHER BOOKS BY
BILLY JOE DAUGHERTY

Knocked Down but Not Out

God Is Not Your Problem

When Life Throws You a Curve

You Can be Healed

**AVAILABLE FROM
DESTINY IMAGE PUBLISHERS**

NO FEAR
Praying the Promises
of Protection

BILLY JOE DAUGHERTY

Please note that Destiny Image's publishing style capitalizes certain pronouns in Scripture that refer to the Father, Son, and Holy Spirit, and may differ from some publishers' styles. Take note that the name satan and related names are not capitalized. We choose not to acknowledge him, even to the point of violating grammatical rules.

DESTINY IMAGE® PUBLISHERS, INC.

P.O. Box 310, Shippensburg, PA 17257-0310

"Speaking to the Purposes of God for this Generation and for the Generations to Come."

This book and all other Destiny Image, Revival Press, Mercy Place, Fresh Bread, Destiny Image Fiction, and Treasure House books are available at Christian bookstores and distributors worldwide.

For a U.S. bookstore nearest you, call **1-800-722-6774.**

For more information on foreign distributors, call **717-532-3040.**

Reach us on the Internet: **www.destinyimage.com.**

ISBN 10: 0-7684-2661-8

ISBN 13: 978-0-7684-2661-8

For Worldwide Distribution, Printed in the U.S.A.

1 2 3 4 5 6 7 8 9 10 11 / 12 11 10 09 08

CONTENTS

ENDORSEMENT

The fear of terror grips the hearts of all Americans. Is there an answer? Pastor Billy Joe Daugherty has written a bold and definitive answer in his latest book *No Fear*. I highly recommend this book to you.

—John Hagee
Senior Pastor, Cornerstone Church
San Antonio, Texas

INTRODUCTION

The terrorism that once plagued other nations took on new meaning as America's own borders were infiltrated in a profound way in 2001 by the terror attacks on New York and Washington. Shooting rampages at schools and college campuses have sent shockwaves of fear and panic through our nation like never before. Today the word *terror* has become a buzzword in America and a source of anxiety among many. Regardless of the method of wickedness, it has robbed innocence and stirred up vulnerability as people wonder, *What's next?*

In ministering to people over the course of thirty-three plus years, I've come to a realization that terror is not only found somewhere in some distant city or nation, but it can also be found deep inside of people's hearts. Undetected to the natural eye, terror has seized people who had no idea what was coming at them. I've looked into the eyes of people facing fears beyond their imagination as they have found themselves trying to understand why their son or daughter turned to drugs or an immoral lifestyle. Fear of the unknown is like a cancer, eating away at life and preventing its victims from properly functioning in society. The word *cancer* or *malignant* on a doctor's report has been known to cause feelings of panic and anxiety in many who have received such a diagnosis. Caught off guard and shaken to the core, patients have had to re-establish their footing and somehow pull themselves up to deal with the crisis at hand.

While some have faced personal crises, our world is experiencing the shaking of natural disasters which are signs of the last days in which we live. There has been an increase of shaking and tremors in the earth as mighty earthquakes, tsunamis, hurricanes, volcanoes, floods, and tornadoes have claimed thousands of lives, injured countless others, and left people homeless or displaced. The effect of sin upon the earth has been devastating. It seems that the appearing of our Lord and Savior could happen at any possible moment.

How can we have no fear of terror in times like these? Is it truly possible? The shaking will not end soon, for Hebrews 12:25-29 tells us:

> *See that you do not refuse Him who speaks. For if they did not escape who refused Him [Jesus] who spoke on earth, much more shall we not escape if we turn away from Him [Jesus] who speaks from heaven, whose voice then shook the earth; but now He has promised, saying,* **"Yet once more I shake not only the earth, but also heaven."** *Now this, "Yet once more," indicates the removal of those things that are being shaken, as of things that are made, that the things which cannot be shaken may remain. Therefore, since we are receiving a kingdom which cannot be shaken, let us have grace, by which we may serve God acceptably with reverence and godly fear. For our God is a consuming fire.*

It is clear that everything that can be shaken will be shaken, but those who know their God will not be moved (see Ps. 62:6). It is important for you to have God's wisdom and stability to be victorious through these coming days. We have not been left here to be swallowed up in fear and terror. We have been brought to this earth for a purpose in this specific time in history.

I want to encourage you to do everything you can to draw near to the Lord in these days—in your personal life, in your walk with the Lord, in Bible reading, in daily prayer time, and in church attendance. Reading of the Word of God is powerful, and I challenge you to read it out loud. Read large portions of it at a time. As you read, I want to encourage you to pray in the early morning, throughout your day, and in the evening. I especially challenge you to establish a time of family prayer, where you can unite and read the Word of God, pray, testify, and share together.

The message of "no fear" is not just for you, but it is also for your children and grandchildren. Isaiah 54:13-14 says, "All your children shall be taught by the Lord, and great shall be the peace of your children. In righteousness you shall be established; you shall be far from oppression, for you shall not fear; and from terror, for it shall not come near you." It's time to get rid of nightmares, fear, and anxiety in our homes and in our land. The principles in this book can set you free from the power of fear to control and manipulate you in your future. If the Lord tarries, we have a job to do unlike any in history. As the world reels in chaos and confusion, we do not have to succumb to the rising fears and worry in the land. We can rise up, take our places of leadership, and finish the course that Jesus began.

Chapter 1

TAKE A STAND AGAINST FEAR

Fear not for I am with you (Isaiah 41:10).

The year was 1973. I was in my early twenties and married to my college sweetheart. Sharon and I excitedly moved into our "new" place—an old, one-room garage apartment renting for $65 a month (bills and bugs included). It was all our college budget would allow. We had each other, and we were in love. Life couldn't have been better.

The day we moved into this apartment, we were greeted by a next door neighbor. "Welcome to the neighborhood," he said. He went on to inform us: "Yesterday the neighbor next door had their house broken into and all of their furniture stolen, and, oh, by the way, the apartment house down the street has a lot of drug people in and out of that place, but we're glad you're here!" Wow! What a welcome!

The country was still at war in Vietnam at that time, and news commentators and government leaders began talking about the economic crash coming to the United States. Even the ministers were preaching about it, warning us to get prepared.

About this time, I came across a book about the coming economic crash. Page after page affirmed that America was headed for a financial disaster.

Even though Sharon and I had heard and memorized a few Scriptures about God taking care of us, I became focused on what the authorities and this author had to say about the economy. The author warned there would be a rush on the grocery stores and the shelves would be emptied, leaving Americans without food for who knew how long. Even ministers were trying to guide the people by telling us about the different types of dried foods that could be stored for long periods of time. The more I thought about this dreaded situation, the more worried I became. The financial forecasters painted a grim picture. Fear of not being able to take care of my new bride and myself started to grip me.

All I remember thinking was, *We have to somehow survive this thing that's coming to America!* I imagined that money was going to be scarce and food was going to be even harder to come by. Where does a young husband go to get survival basics for what we were obviously going to face? As the head of this household, I needed a plan. We began to add two bags of dried beans to our already meager $13.63 average weekly grocery bill. To supplement our dried bean stash, I began to wonder, *What kind of food is available that is cheap or even free?* Ah-hah. I had an idea.

The public park always had nuts littering the ground. I knew nuts were nutritious, full of protein. They probably stored well without refrigeration, which was a good thing in case electricity was also endangered by whatever was headed our way. I mean, who knew how bad this could get? I can admit now that I didn't know much about the different kinds of nuts that grew on trees, especially the ones that are abundant at the public parks. I thought most nuts were basically the same. But I can tell you from experience, that's not true.

I told Sharon, "Come on," and we headed to the park. We each filled two grocery sacks of the nuts. It seemed like there was more than enough for anyone to pick up. What a deal. When we brought them home, Sharon toasted some in the oven. When they cooled off, she and I each took a bite and got the surprise of our lives. These were okay for the squirrels, but *acorns* would never do for us! They tasted terrible!

With the taste of roasted acorn still in my mouth, I came to myself. I said to Sharon, "God has to have a better way to keep us alive through whatever is coming." And I can assure you, He did. As I began focusing on God's promises from His Word that He would meet our needs, peace settled in me once again. No matter what would come our way, we were going to make it. And make it we did. God always provided for us. By the way, the crash we feared did not come. The following summer, in 1974, we began to hear ministers who spoke about living by faith in the promises of God. Our worldview and our way of thinking were transformed as a result of hearing the message of faith and living by the Word of God.

Fear, if not conquered, will continue to repeat its vicious cycle. Moving the clock forward a few years, many may remember in 1999, during the time of Y2K, that people became fearful about what would happen at the turn of this century. There were some who wrote books that fueled the spirit of fear in people. Today we can see that we made that turn into the 21st century, and our society did not go under as predicted. This does not mean there couldn't be difficult economic times in the future, but those who live by faith in God's Word will see God's provision no matter what happens around them.

FEAR AND ITS FRIENDS

Dread, foreboding, torment, apprehension, anxiety, terror—if fear was a gang leader, these would be his faithful followers who obey his every order to torment and traumatize. They lurk and wait and watch for an opportune time to catch people off guard. They don't play favorites either. Whether you're a strong athlete, a reputable world leader, a businessperson, a stay-at-home wife and mother, or a highly-decorated soldier, you must stand against fear to preserve your destiny, your very life. Fear has a target, and that target is people. Even some of our most powerful leaders have had to confront and conquer fear's debilitating control.

President Franklin D. Roosevelt, for instance, knew something of the fear that grips humankind. He was elected at a time when the depression was in full swing and the American people felt hopeless. It seemed that their hopes were shattered at every turn by the financial straits facing them. Those with life savings held in banks had become penniless overnight. In his inaugural address of 1933, FDR knew he needed to reignite the passion and dream of victory or America would find itself worse off than it already was. He spoke of fear as if he was personally acquainted with its deadly workings: "...let me assert my firm belief that the only thing we have to fear is fear itself—nameless, unreasoning, unjustified terror which paralyzes needed efforts to convert retreat into advance."[1] FDR described fear as a power that cripples those who could otherwise have the power to fight back.

TERRORISM UNVEILED

Fast forward to the world we live in today. Prior to September 11, 2001, no one watched the news to find out whether the homeland security alert status was on yellow, orange, or red. As a matter of fact, there was no department of homeland security before then. We'd never heard of Osama bin Laden, and we weren't concerned about terrorism. That was something that happened in other parts of the world—not in our Westernized society.

The whole idea of terrorism is to put fear in people and then to manipulate through that fear. But make no mistake: terror is not limited to nations and those "out there." It can come at a person when he or she hears the latest medical research statistics about a deadly disease. That feeling of fear and its negative thoughts must be resisted with the truth of God's Word.

Who is the original terrorist? It's satan. Since pride caused his fall from the throne of God, he has been at war with mankind ever since. There is no redemption for him as there is for man. When Jesus, the Son of God, was raised from the dead, as Colossians 2:15 says, "Having disarmed principalities and powers, He made a public spectacle of them, triumphing over them in it." Jesus defused satan's power through the cross and resurrection, so now his only plan of attack is through lies, fear, and manipulations of truth, always trying to disprove what Jesus has already done.

THE WAY FEAR WORKS

Fear begins with an imagination. Someone can get all worked up over a thought that travels through the mind. The body can even begin to feel the effects of that fear—heart racing, sweaty palms, or irrational thoughts. When I feared the impending economic crash back in the '70s, I could imagine us going to the grocery store and finding no food on the shelves, and I eventually began voicing and acting upon that fear.

Fear, once it enters the mind, then gets people to start talking about it. When people fear flying in airplanes, they will many times feed that fear by telling others, "Oh, flying always scares me." They don't realize that, by voicing their fears, they're digging a deeper pit from which they will have to climb. When you imagine something and then start talking about it, you will begin to believe it. There are people who firmly believe their fears. They'll look you straight in the eye and tell you how scared they are, and they believe it with all their heart.

Our beliefs then lead to actions. Someone who fears flying and has voiced that over and over eventually may find a need to travel by airplane. At that point, fear has become stronger in this individual than the reality of a safe plane ride. With tightly clenched fists and labored breathing, they may endure that trip, but it's definitely not enjoyable for them.

THE WAY FAITH WORKS

Now let's take a look on the brighter side. I want to introduce a better way, a way to walk through life above fear and terror. It is the walk by faith. Fear attracts the works of the enemy, but faith draws the power of God. Faith is a trust, an assurance in God's ability to take you through whatever He sends your way. Faith works exactly opposite of fear. Whereas fear is negative, faith is positive. Sharon's mom has a plaque on her wall that reads, "Fear knocked at the door, faith answered, and no one was there." Fear opens the door to lying imaginations of the enemy. Jonah 2:8 says, "They that observe lying vanities forsake their own mercy" (KJV). Faith has imaginations, too. It believes the Word of God with the heart. It draws on what God said instead of on fearful thoughts and anxieties. How do you build faith in God's ability to keep you safe from all harm? It begins by listening to and reading the written words of God (see Rom. 10:17). Jesus Himself is the Word of God that was made flesh (see John 1:14).

As you listen to the Word of God, you are listening to Him speak to you personally. When you begin to speak God's Word (His promises), you give voice to your faith. The Bible is full of encouragement, direction, and protection for your life. You will begin imagining yourself strong, capable, and ready for whatever comes your way. That's because you've been thinking and talking about how great God is. You can't possibly read His Word and meditate on the Scriptures without realizing that you have a big God who delights in seeing you accomplish His will in the earth. From there you take steps that positively affect your destiny. You start seeking God's will and finding His purposes for your life. And as you do, you go wherever He says and do whatever He tells you to do.

You and I must make up our minds that we are not going to let fear get inside of us, no matter what happens in the earth. We are going to counter the attacks of the enemy with God's Word and live above the fear. To make it through whatever comes our way, we must walk by faith all the way. The Bible says in Galatians 3:11, "The just shall live by faith." Faith requires us to not live by our feelings, because feelings can change regularly. We choose to live by God's Word (His Scriptures), because His Word is stable and established. God's Word has the answer for every fear or torment that you face—whether it's external or internal.

IS THERE NOT A CAUSE?

One of my early childhood experiences with fear left an indelible mark on my memory. I've never liked it when the schoolyard bully got the upper hand over some unsuspecting new kid. It always bothered me. I always thought, *Who does he think he is?* Maybe that's because I had my own run-in with a bully when I was about seven years old. It made quite an impression on me.

This guy lived down the street from me and wouldn't leave me alone—always taunting and making fun of me. That bully was a "Goliath" in my life. I guess he figured he could pick on me and get away with it since he was bigger and older. I came home and mentioned to my dad what the guy had done. He called in my two older brothers. "Boys," he told them, "get the baseball bats and go down there and talk to that guy with Billy

Joe." Wow! I will never forget how confident I felt walking down the middle of the road that day with my two older brothers as we were sent on assignment from my dad to that guy's house. Amazingly, when we knocked on his door that afternoon, the bully was very apologetic. We didn't have to use the baseball bats on him after all.

When David faced Goliath in First Samuel 17, he was shocked to think that no one would fight this mocking giant. This army of trained men were not only frightened by Goliath's words, but they also couldn't imagine anyone else being "man" enough to silence the threat across the valley. Fear had shut down their ability to see past the threats to their survival. Even the country's leader, the king, was too afraid to aggressively take out this foe. But David, a man who had spent much time with the Lord and knew His character, posed a defining question to his fellow Israelites: "Is there not a cause?" (1 Sam. 17:29). In our own language, this is what I think that question meant: "Doesn't anybody have the courage to stand up against this giant? Don't you understand that we're in covenant with God and that giant has no covenant? Aren't our wives and children worth the fight? We have every reason to fight and win against this threat to our people. God is on our side!"

This is the crux of what I want you to understand for your own life. Threats may come and go, but bowing down to the fear of those threats gives the enemy (satan) access to run over your life and hinder you from fulfilling God's purpose. Fears may come, but as author and evangelist Joyce Meyer says,

> When God said, "Fear not," He did not mean don't feel fear. What He meant was, "When you feel fear you know that I am with you and I will never leave you nor

forsake you. And you step out and you do what you believe I've told you to do no matter how you feel."[2]

Everyone feels fear, but each of us decides whether we're going to accept the fear or reject it. Living above fear means not cowering before it or bowing to its demands. Give fear no place in your life.

Is there not a cause? There was a cause for my dad to send my older brothers with me that day as a show of strength against his youngest son's adversary. His unspoken message to the bully was: *Don't mess with my son!* That's the way our Father God feels about us when the enemy, satan, comes with his threats and imaginations of hopelessness. God wants us to realize that He is greater than satan and that we are in covenant relationship with Him. If God is for us, then who can prevail against us? (See Romans 8:31.)

When the Israelites believed that their freedom would soon be extinguished through slavery to their enemies, David, who understood his covenant relationship with God, became a confident warrior that day to change the course of Israel's history. There is a cause for you to stand strong against the fear of terror that is trying to engulf people in these days. It's your turn to fight the giant of fear to preserve your destiny and your children's future. Your history is at stake.

ENDNOTES

1. Franklin D. Roosevelt, "Only Thing We Have to Fear Is Fear Itself," Inaugural Address, March 4, 1933, as published in Samuel Rosenman, ed., *The Public Papers of Franklin D. Roosevelt, Volume Two: The Year of Crisis, 1933* (New York: Random House, 1938), 11-16, available at

History Matters, http://historymatters.gmu.edu/d/5057 (accessed 6 March 2007).

2. Joyce Meyer, *Be an Eagle, Not a Chicken* (Tulsa, OK: Victory Christian Center, March 4, 2007).

Chapter 2

KNOWING THE ENEMY

I sought the Lord, and He heard me, and delivered me from all my fears (Psalm 34:4).

In the days and weeks that followed the terrorist attacks in 2001, Americans tried to grasp who the enemy was and why they would want to kill innocent people. Our Western mindset could not comprehend such atrocious acts of murder against a peaceful society. It had not even occurred to most Americans that we could be the target of such an attack. Terror took on new meaning for us as we saw firsthand what it could do.

One of the most basic fundamentals of war became America's mission: Know your enemy. The more you know your enemy, the higher your success rate for defeating him. That particular aspect became a challenge for Western ideology as we learned that our enemy was not bound by a country or land. The phrase "sleeper cells" was coined as we began to understand that the enemy could possibly live among us, waiting for orders from their masters who dictated when and where their missions of terror were to take place. As Christians, we understand that the enemy behind all terrorism is satan. Jesus said in Luke 10:19, "Behold, I give you the authority...over all the power of the enemy, and nothing shall by any means hurt you." That power is in Jesus and in His Name.

WHAT IS THE PURPOSE OF FEAR AND TERROR?

By understanding both fear and terror, we are better able to combat satan's missions for them in our lives. By definition, *fear* means "an unpleasant often strong emotion caused by anticipation or awareness of danger."[1] In Webster's 1828 Dictionary, it says that "Fear expresses less apprehension than *dread*, and dread less than *terror* and *fright*. The force of this passion, beginning with the most moderate degree, may be thus expressed: *fear, dread, terror, fright*."[2] So fear has a downward spiral toward terror. *Terror* is defined in Webster's 1828 dictionary as "a state of intense fear; violent dread; fright; fear that agitates the body and mind."[3] In a more current dictionary, *terror* denotes "violent or destructive acts (as bombing) committed by groups in order to intimidate a population or government into granting their demands."[4]

The intense emotion of fear carries with it a strong desire to run from the danger that it senses or anticipates or to fight against it. For those who fear heights, the longing to be on the ground will strongly motivate them to take the quickest exit by way of elevator or stairs. They perceive that the safest place for them is the exact opposite of where they are.

Fear can also paralyze people, keeping them from moving forward or changing direction. That happened to the children of Israel when they were sent on a mission from God to spy out the land of Canaan. They had miraculously been delivered from slavery in Egypt for the purpose of going back into the land promised to their forefathers (see Exod. 12:40-42). As Numbers 13:2 records, the Lord said to Moses, "Send men to spy out the land of Canaan, which I am giving to the children of Israel." Here we find their purpose—to have the property that the Lord was intending to give them.

When the report came back concerning the land, the men confirmed it was everything God said it would be. They brought back samples of the fruit and their eyewitness reports of how it was "flowing with milk and honey" (see Num. 13:27), or in today's language, "a great place to live." Yet the land would not be taken without a battle. That's the part that caused great concern for ten of the twelve spies. Their description of the men who lived in the land brought fear on the Israelites, and they couldn't see past their own weaknesses. They pulled back on their mission to take the land because of how they compared themselves to the enemy.

Caleb and Joshua, however, had a different take on the situation. They had spied out the land with the other men, but they were determined to fight and take the land. What was the difference in their perceptions? It was this: The Lord said He was giving the Israelites the land. That settled the issue for Caleb and Joshua. It didn't matter who their enemy was. It mattered only that the Lord said He had given it to them.

It is not always the strong and mighty who necessarily get a job done. It is the courageous and determined who follow through on a mission. Sometimes the ones who are least likely in the natural to win against an enemy are the very ones who walk away as victors. They rise up to take the lead when everyone else is too tired or weak in faith. They stay on their God-ordained purpose and win out in the end. These are individuals who know their mission, know their God, and are not easily swayed from their objective by bad reports. This is the same positive attitude that we must adapt in order to counteract the bad news that daily floods our media.

FEARS THAT PEOPLE FACE

Twenty-four hours a day, news inundates our airwaves, making sure we know everything that could possibly be happening around the world. From the Internet to cable news shows, we are bombarded by tragedy after calamity after threat. But the news stations are not the only communicators of fears. There are fears between ethnic groups because of their past history. After 9/11, Americans began fearing neighbors and co-workers who were Muslims. People became cautious and suspicious when they traveled on public transportation systems and saw men and women of Middle Eastern descent. Recent events had put doubt in their minds as they wondered if that bus or plane was to be the next target. This same scenario can be replicated in any ethnic group where there has been past history of racial prejudice. Unspoken tensions exist. Everyone is watching their backs. That fear stems from distrust of the other racial group, and it can cause accusations of wrongdoing just because of the color of one's skin.

Fear has also gripped some people because of a diagnosis from a physician or a forecast by a certified public accountant. The day prior to receiving the bad report, life was grand. They had nothing to worry about. Suddenly, however, that same person is faced with a mountain of fear. Such was the case with Darlene, a single parent mom who was suddenly faced with an unexpected tragedy. In the Fall of 2000, Darlene's teenage daughter, Heather, went into a diabetic coma and was pronounced medically dead. Different people came and spoke the Word of God over her. Darlene recounts the story of dealing with the fear of possibly losing her daughter at such a young age:

> I had been speaking Psalm 91 over my children and family every day. When Heather had gone into a coma and then was on life support, my first thought was negative: *This is it!* And then God spoke within my heart and said, "You don't have to receive this. Are you going to fight or are you going to give up?"

And that's the choice we have. In everything we go through, we can either give up (that's the easiest way) or we can fight. Darlene went on to say,

> And I knew that this was my time to fight. I had been to Bible college, and I thought, *This is the big fight.* I just had to dig in and do those things that I believed. I remembered the words of men and women of God that came back to me at that time, giving me the strength and courage to stand.

The doctors were saying it was over and were giving Darlene time to accept the situation. However, God was encouraging Darlene to stand in faith and see a miracle happen.

> We spoke the Word of God over her. I would stand over her, lay hands on her, and command her body to

do what the Word of God said it was going to do. She was going to rise up, and she was going to be whole. Others came and did the same. The doctors told me that her charts said she was clinically dead, but Heather came out of that coma. I heard the nurse say, "She's trying to communicate," and the doctor said, "No, she's not." His way of looking at it was that she is never coming out of the coma. Either she was going to be brain dead or she was going to die. That was it. But she started communicating.

Before Heather went into the coma, the American presidency had still not been decided because of a vote recount between George W. Bush and Al Gore. When she woke up from the coma, the doctor questioned her as though he was trying to find something wrong with her. To his amazement, she answered all his questions without any problem. The last question he asked her was, "Who's the president of the United States?" And Heather said, "Nobody knows that." She had remembered before she went into the coma that the presidency was undecided. The doctor just looked at her and walked away because he knew that he had seen something that was not taught in the medical books and was not taught in college. He had to recognize that our God reigns.

Today Heather is thriving as a healthy wife and mother, thanks to the ones who fought thoughts of fear and wouldn't give up on her.

I understand the power that fears and phobias exert over people, and I don't discount their feelings at those times of extreme distress. But any way you look at it, that's not God's best for people. God has a better way. The fallen world that we live in is not supposed to be dictating to us how we should live and what we should feel. Man has to be set free from this demonic stronghold that has worked to ruin and wreck lives.

FEAR IS A SPIRIT

Second Timothy 1:7 clearly tells us that "God has not given us a spirit of fear, but of power and of love and of a sound mind." Fear is sent by satan, and he wants to control and manipulate people's lives. The spirit of fear brings torment to the mind. Sometimes you'll find that the same fears that Grandma or Dad had are the same ones that the next generation faces. That's a generational curse that has a foothold in the family because it's never been dealt with. People have learned to accommodate it in their lives and have made room for it in their schedules.

We had to combat a spirit of fear when we went into Pakistan to hold evangelistic meetings in 2005. The timing of the crusade was phenomenal. It was planned months in advance with our contacts in that country. Little did we know that they would suffer one of the worst earthquakes in history a few days before we were scheduled to arrive. In fact, one of our team members was there when the earthquake hit. We continued with our plans to be there to bring hope immediately after that devastation. Along with the natural disaster, there had been persecution from radical terrorists toward Christianity in that country. The Pakistani Christian leaders took the proper precautions to guard us in light of all that had happened in their country. The local people coordinated the security for us, and they hired a group of people who happened to be Muslims. They had been trained in the military and then formed a security organization. We were surrounded by Muslim men with AK47 machine guns.

I thought about it while we were there—that we never had a spirit of fear in us during that whole time, but we could tell that those men who were guarding us were dealing with fear. Our prayer was that the Lord was going to enter their hearts, and we believe that happened. They were very receptive and received us with open arms. They were eager to stand with us so that we could take pictures with them, and they wanted to do the same with us. We knew that we had been sent by God to do His work of harvesting souls in that nation.

Even though it is important to use our common sense in taking protective precautions, a gun doesn't make you free from fear. A lock doesn't make you free from fear. Neither does a dog, a light, or a security force. It's when you decide that enough is enough that you're ready to be free and never look back. You begin to change the way you think. You guard your thoughts from feeding upon negative information all the time. You choose to believe God's Word: "Fear not, for I am with you; be not dismayed, for I am your God. I will strengthen you, yes, I will help you, I will uphold you with My righteous right hand" (Isa. 41:10).

ENDNOTES

1. *Merriam-Webster's Collegiate Dictionary*, 11th ed., s.v. "Fear."

2. Noah Webster, *American Dictionary of the English Language,* 1828 ed, s.v. "Fear."

3. *Ibid.,* s.v. "Terror."

4. *Merriam-Webster's Collegiate Dictionary,* 11th ed., s.v. "Terror."

Chapter 3

GOD IS A GOOD GOD

*The Lord is my light and my salvation; whom shall I
fear? The Lord is the strength of my life; of whom shall I
be afraid?* (Psalm 27:1)

In the religious background that I grew up in, when we would
go to the hospital to visit sick and dying people, we would
"remember" them in our prayers. That's what I told them: "I'll
remember you in my prayers." All I did was remember them,
because I really didn't think God would heal them. I knew He
could heal them, but I sure didn't know if He *would*. As I visited a friend in the hospital, I thought, *Why can't God just heal
him?*

Many years ago, healing evangelist Oral Roberts received
much criticism when he proclaimed, "God is a good God!"
That was a revelation that the religious world had not considered and could hardly accept. But many of us caught hold of
that and saw the workings of God in a whole new way. I began
learning about how God healed people, and I have seen Him
use me to minister to them. God is a good God!

So why are we talking about how God is good in a book
about having no fear? Because if you don't believe God is good,

you will be pulled into the grip of fear in situations that you face. Up until the time when I heard that it was God's will to heal people, I never prayed for anyone to be healed. No one wanted to fight against God's will, and since we didn't know what His will was, we just assumed that if the sick lived, He wanted them healed. If they died, then we assumed He wanted them to leave this life earlier than we thought. What you believe about God's character will either cause you to fight for your God-given rights or cause you to retreat into the *que sera, sera* (whatever will be, will be) mode. Knowing that God's will for you is good is the beginning of standing against fear. An exemplary image of His "good will" is depicted in the book of Genesis through the life God created for Adam and Eve.

THE BATTLE IS ON

The Garden of Eden must have really been something: lions and bears as tame as common house pets, Adam and Eve walking and talking with God in the middle of the day, no bills due and no retirement funds to put away, no lumps or bumps on their bodies to cause concern, and no wondering who moved in across the street and if the new neighbors could be trusted around their children. Sounds like the good life, doesn't it? Well, it was. Adam and Eve were in a place where the glory of God covered them. That glory made everything available to them that they would need on this earth. It was all at their disposal and under their authority. God had lavishly given them the best that this earth had to offer. There wasn't anything that God withheld from them in the Garden. Well, except for the tree of the knowledge of good and evil. It was simple. God said they could eat from any tree in the garden except that one. That might have been a fairly easy command to keep, but there was a deceiver in their midst—satan disguised as a serpent (see Gen. 3).

We could talk all day about what Adam and Eve shouldn't have done and how they could have handled the whole situation differently. We can surmise what they must have been thinking and why they did what they did. But that won't change anything. Mankind was forever marred because of Adam and Eve's decision to eat the fruit from the forbidden tree. Immediately, God said to satan that the day would come when the seed of woman (meaning Jesus, a virgin birth, since the seed comes from the male and not the female) shall bruise satan's head (satan's power or authority over man) and satan would bruise his heel (meaning the physical suffering and death Jesus would go through) (see Gen. 3:15). Then hundreds of years later, Isaiah prophesied of this virgin birth (see Isa. 7:14). Matthew later recounts Isaiah's words being fulfilled in Matthew 1:18-25.

The Word that was with God in the beginning and was God (see John 1:1-2) "was made flesh and dwelt among us, (and we beheld His glory, the glory as of the one and only begotten of the Father,) full of grace and truth" (John 1:14 KJV). The Son of God willingly gave up His position in Heaven to enter our world. His life was not taken from Him as some suppose; He *chose* to pay the price for man's sin through His death on the cross. He was physically tortured and beaten for your sake and mine (see Isa. 53:3-6; 1 Pet. 2:24). To the amazement of the Roman soldiers, who were watching the tomb where He was laid, this man of humility was then resurrected three days after He had died (see 1 Cor.15:3-8).

The reason Jesus came to this earth and suffered as He did is summed up in a familiar verse, John 3:16: "For God so loved the world that He gave His only begotten Son, that whoever believes in Him should not perish but have everlasting life." Love was the reason that God sent His Son. And the following verse in that passage, which is probably lesser known, is the answer to what some people question: "For God did not send His Son into the world to condemn the world, but that the world through Him might be saved" (John 3:17). By believing in your heart that God raised Jesus from the dead and then speaking (confessing) that with your mouth, the Bible says you will be saved (see Romans 10:9-10). You may ask, "Saved from what?" You're saved from the lake of fire and eternal damnation and saved from being a slave to sin.

I was a church member for many years but didn't have a close relationship with Jesus. I didn't know Him intimately and personally. If someone had asked me, "Do you believe in Jesus?" I would have said, "Yeah," because I was not an atheist. I had heard about Christ; I knew the stories. I was in church and Sunday school, and I was president of my church's youth group, but I didn't have that intimate, personal relationship with Him. I remember one Sunday when I was a teenager that a young man about my age from another church came to give a testimony at our church. He talked about having a relationship with Jesus. It shook me. I remember that I was sitting in the middle of the section in that part of the church, and I just stared at the guy, because I knew he wasn't trying to impress anyone. He was just very simple and straightforward, but he talked like he really knew Jesus and like Jesus talked to him. It wasn't long after that I accepted Jesus as my personal Lord and Savior. That's the best decision I have ever made. The message of the cross and the victory Jesus won through His resurrection have directed the entire course of my life since then, but that doesn't mean that it has always been easy.

As Christians, we are called to carry out God's will on the earth, which makes us in direct opposition to the desire of satan. The war is on. Satan has lost the battle for our souls, but he still attempts to steal, kill, and destroy us through whatever means he can (see John 10:10). Evil is his nature. But don't get God and the devil mixed up. There's a simple formula I learned many years ago that helps me to keep it straight: God = good; devil = evil. If something is good and for your benefit, then it's from God. If it's evil and causes destruction, then it's from the devil. God and the devil do not change places; God remains a doer of good, and the devil continues to work his evil deeds. Further, God doesn't use the devil to teach us. When bad things happen, there are reasons. Somewhere the enemy broke through. We must be willing to seek God and know how the enemy operates so that we can stop him.

GOD'S WAYS

After thirty-three years of marriage, Sharon and I can just about finish each others' sentences. We have come to know one another's thoughts, ways, and feelings on certain subjects and situations. That oneness is a result of our spending time together and communicating on an intimate level. The same process of learning God's ways and His character comes by spending time with Him. Through His Word and His spirit, which will always agree, we find the will of God.

Many people say that evil circumstances can somehow produce good for us. For each person who says that something good has come out of evil, you can find many others who say something more evil has come out of it. One person may turn to the Lord in a situation, while others turn away from God and become hardened, turning to drugs, alcohol, and immorality. If evil automatically produced good, then we would see good all over the world, and there would not be any more evil.

Others have been ingrained with a negative view of God. Their concept is that God is against them and that He is using bad things in order to develop them. People wouldn't think of turning their children over to a murderer, a liar, or a thief to teach them character, yet somehow that concept of God's character has been maligned. Our heavenly Father has given the Holy Spirit, the Word of God, the gifts of the Spirit, and the blood of Jesus to help us. Why would He use the devil to teach His children? If bad things were all sent from God to teach us and to develop our character, then everybody in extremely poor regions would be saved right now because there are horrible, devastating things that are happening to millions of people in those countries. The truth is that God is not the author of evil in the world. Evil things happen because of the devil, the fall of man in the Garden of Eden, the curse that came to the earth, and the sins of mankind.

Any good that comes out of an evil situation does not come from the evil. It comes from God as a result of people turning to Him through repentance, faith, and prayer. First

Thessalonians 5:18 says, "In everything give thanks...." It doesn't say to give thanks *for* everything. But *in* everything you can give thanks because God hasn't changed. Where Ephesians 5:20 says, "Giving thanks always for all things unto God..." (KJV), it is understood in the context of Scripture that the writer, Paul, was referring to being thankful for all the good things God had done, all of His promises and benefits.

In the very beginning, there was no evil, and Jesus brought no evil when He came into the earth. Evil has never been a part of God's plan for your past, present, or future. God has not changed His will. Sin, sickness, accidents, criminals, fear, and bondage each represent various forms of evil. If it is evil, God wants you free from it. Jesus prayed for His disciples before He went to the cross: "I do not pray that You should take them out of the world, but that You should keep them from the evil one" (John 17:15). Notice here that Jesus wasn't saying that when they got to Heaven there would be no evil. He was talking about keeping us from the evil one while we are here on this earth.

GOD IS WITH YOU

God tells us over and over in His Word to "fear not." Isaiah 41:10 is a particular "fear not" that I want to draw your attention to: "Fear not, for I am with you; be not dismayed, for I am your God. I will strengthen you, Yes, I will help you, I will uphold you with My righteous right hand." He is *Emmanuel*, "God with us." Rest in knowing that He is here for you. He has chosen to make His place where you are. Shake off being discouraged or downhearted. Even if plans didn't turn out the way you thought they would, God is still here. He is an ever-present help in time of trouble. The Prince of Peace (Jesus) wants you to keep your mind clear and sharp through whatever you're going through. The strength and help that you need are found only in Him. As you lean on Him and His ability to lead you in your decisions at this very time, you will be encouraged by the perfect way He guides you. When you feel like you have the world on your shoulders, He says that He's the One who's holding you up. If He holds the universe up, He can surely hold you up. Whatever it is, it's not too big for God.

Isaiah 41:11 addresses those who may come against you: "Behold, all those who were incensed against you shall be ashamed and disgraced; they shall be as nothing, and those who strive with you shall perish." Over the years, there have been times that I've actually felt sorry for people who came against us. I just said, "You don't know what's about to happen to your life." That's why we don't have to get upset or fight back. We pray for them and bless them because they just set in motion a spiritual law. If a person comes out against the righteous and becomes a weapon formed against the righteous, God will bring that individual down. Once that gets inside of you, then you will understand even better Jesus' teaching about how we can love our enemies and pray for those who persecute us (see Luke 6:27-36). We know that God is going to stand up and fight for us. He will deliver us.

When it comes down to it, as we keep looking to Him for our help, we won't even notice those who have desired to harm us. We will say, "They were here a minute, a day, a month ago. Where are they now?" In Isaiah 41:12, it goes on to say, "...Those who war against you shall be as nothing, as a non-existent thing." It will be as if the plot or plan against you never existed. The next verse goes on to declare the essence of who your God is. Not only is He God Almighty, Alpha and Omega, the first and the last, from everlasting to everlasting, the Creator of the universe, but He holds your hand—He's right there with you—and He says to you, "Fear not."

> *For I, the Lord your God, will hold your right hand, saying to you, "Fear not, I will help you"* (Isaiah 41:13).

THE REALLY GOOD SHEPHERD

If you've been at church at all in your life, you've probably heard Psalm 23 at some point. Sometimes people say, "Oh, I know that psalm," and then they rattle it off like it's the Gettysburg Address, having no concept of how that psalm relates to their lives. By nature, sheep need someone who will watch them and look out for what's ahead so that they can be led to safe places. If they can't find enough food as they're grazing with the flock, or if they see a green pasture off at a distance that looks more appealing, then they start going off on their own, looking for food and making themselves vulnerable to attack. They are defenseless animals and easy prey.

Keeping this in mind, consider people as those sheep who need someone to watch over their lives. We need God to tell us, "This is the way." People's stubbornness can get them into trouble and keep them trying to figure out their way on their own. God knows that if we're not satisfied, we'll start to wander off, making us especially susceptible to the attack of the enemy in those lonely places. Staying with the flock (the family of God) puts us in the safest place. Let's look at Psalm 23 from the perspective of God being that ever watchful, diligent

Shepherd who has a responsibility over us to bring us home safely.

If the Lord is your Shepherd, you shall not want. (See Psalm 23:1.) No matter what you need, God is good and in Him there's no lack. You don't have to start looking at other pastures, going off on your own to survive. The grass isn't greener on the other side. Where you are is the best place to be, because "He makes me to lie down in green pastures..." (Ps. 23:2). These aren't the old burned-up, dead places where the food is scarce. No, this is the lush, abundant place in life where you'll desire to be. "He leads me beside still waters" (Ps. 23:2). These are the peaceful, gentle places of life—where you are in the will of God, performing the right job, and enjoying pleasant relationships. Keep in mind: This is where the *good* Shepherd leads.

"He restores my soul..." (Ps. 23:3). God is the Restorer of your soul, not the destroyer. You may have had a calamity or a tragedy, an accident, or something bad that came against your life. Many times people think that God was working against them, attacking them. Some even think that God was trying to teach them some life lesson through it. The Scripture doesn't say, "He breaks the broken heart." It says, "He *heals* the broken-hearted..." (Ps. 147:3). He restores what the enemy has destroyed (see Joel 2:25).

"He leads me in paths of righteousness for His name's sake" (Ps. 23:3). God will always lead us toward right paths and right living because we bear His name. If you take a wrong path or do wrong, repent and get back into submission to Jesus' lordship. If some bad things happened and you got into some unfortunate situations, it wasn't God's fault. He doesn't tempt with evil (see James 1:13-14). But He can help you get back on course with His will if you let Him.

"Yea, though I walk through the valley of the shadow of death, I will fear no evil; for You are with me..." (Ps. 23:4). The valley represents a low time. This could be a time where your emotions feel low. Notice He says the *shadow* of death. A shadow is not the real thing. You may feel like you are going through a dangerous situation or a dangerous time, but remember that the psalmist said you're going "through." You're not staying there. You are coming out to the other side. Best of all, God is with you. He's Almighty, and He will deliver you because you belong to Him. The Psalmist had a revelation of the goodness of God. His expectation of the future was not that something bad was going to destroy him. He knew that God was there for him, and when you have God with you, there is no fear of evil tomorrow. God is going to see you through whatever situation you might face.

We're not walking from a good day to a bad day. No, we must begin to believe that our days are going to go from glory to glory to glory to glory (see 2 Cor. 3:18). When we focus on the negative and think, *Well, this didn't work out, and that didn't happen,* we'll anticipate more bad things coming our way. It's time to break that negative syndrome and to think about God's goodness toward us. In the U.S., despite all the blessings that they have, people often have a bad day over a hangnail! Or they think that their whole day is messed up because they didn't get the right parking place. You have far too much to give thanks for to get focused on the negative.

"Your rod and your staff, they comfort me" (Ps. 23:4). His rod is His Word; His staff is His Spirit. He has provided them for us in order to keep us going in the right direction. When He needs to correct or discipline us with the aid of His Word and instruct us by His Spirit, then we are at peace, knowing that we belong to His flock; for "...God deals with you as with sons; for what son is there whom a father does not chasten?" (Heb. 12:7). We all need God's correction at times. If we receive His correction, we grow and become stronger and more discerning. If we don't receive His correction, we will end up walking through painful circumstances again. He uses His Word and His Spirit to warn us and guide us for our benefit.

"You prepare a table before me in the presence of my enemies..." (Ps. 23:5). Even as your enemies are watching, God is providing for you. They watch when you have peace in the midst of the storms of life. They wonder how you seem to have what you need when they know you don't have much in your natural situation. There's no need to go anywhere else than where He provides because God always gives what is beneficial and satisfying. Since there are no enemies in Heaven, it is obvious that the Lord is talking about these blessings while we're here on the earth. "You anoint my head with oil..." (Ps. 23:5). That oil represents the presence and power of the Holy Spirit. Oil was poured upon Aaron the high priest, which was a symbol of God's anointing on him. The anointing oil of God destroys any yoke of the enemy's oppression (see Isa. 10:27). The anointing flows when we begin to worship God. His anointing actually abides within our lives to instruct us and flow through us to others (see 1 John 2:27).

"...My cup runs over" (Ps. 23:5). After He fills us up, we have more than enough to give to others. Life in Jesus is overflowing with all His blessings. Psalm 23:6 is an expectation of what will follow the person who submits to the Good

Shepherd's leading: "Surely goodness and mercy shall follow me all the days of my life; and I will dwell in the house of the Lord forever." That's where you can be–with goodness and mercy wherever you go, dwelling in the house of the Lord forever. The goodness of God is not only following us, it surrounds us.

Are you getting a picture yet of how good God is? When you begin to talk of God's goodness, "God, You've been good. Thank You, Lord, for Your goodness," you draw those benefits toward you. As you focus on the goodness of God, you will see that His goodness is far above whatever has happened in your past, whatever's happening right now, and whatever's in store for your future. You are the sheep of His pasture, and He is caring for you. You have no need to fear.

GOD WILL MAKE A WAY OF ESCAPE

Because God is good, there is a way of escape for you from every wicked situation. Look for it. Expect it. He will make it plain to you so that you cannot miss it. Tim Veldstra was at the World Trade Center, Building Number Two, on September 11, 2001. He was a member of our church at the time and has a remarkable story of how God made a way of escape for him.

It is 8:45 A.M. on September 11, 2001. I am on the 61st floor of the World Trade Center Number Two in New York City looking out the break room window at the Statue of Liberty. What a view! This is something I need to show my wife and twelve-year-old daughter, along with the other sites I've seen in New York City.

I've been in New York for three days now as part of a three-week business trip.

I hear a boom but think nothing of it, but then I see a shower of paper falling from the sky above me, much of it on fire. I walk to the west side of the building to the room I just came from and spot a broken window. Many windows are broken from the explosion. I stare for a moment at the window, not understanding the significance of the event. I turn back to the break room and pour myself a cup of coffee.

Within minutes we are told to evacuate using the stairs. I sneak back to my room with the broken window and grab my briefcase, and I head for the stairs with 300 others from my floor. The staircase is crowded. We add more people at every floor. Someone pushes on my back for me to move faster, but I can only move as fast as the crowd. I let these two girls pass me. I see the fear on their faces, but I am not afraid. I know God is with me.

As we go down, we pass people who have stopped to rest. Men are waiting with women who are struggling with the pace down the stairs. After we pass the 41st floor, the building rocks back and forth as the second plane rockets through our tower. I hear screaming and shouting. "Keep moving! Keep moving!" they shout, as they begin to press against me. I say a short prayer, "Lord, I know You will get me out of this."

With the sudden press of people, I consider getting back on a floor so I'm not pushed down the stairs by the crowd, but others shout to stop pushing. We continue down, and I notice the air is stuffy. I open the door at each floor as I walk by for a rush of fresh air. The air gets smoky at the seventh floor and gets worse as we get closer to the bottom. Many men are using their shirts as a mask to filter the smoke. Twenty-five minutes after we start down the stairs, we reach Ground Zero. Rescue workers direct us to a safe exit. We're not allowed to stop until we are blocks from the Towers.

I turn around to look at huge holes in both towers, but I have no idea what has caused the explosions. Someone screams, and I see two people falling from the Towers. The buildings are so tall that it's hard to recognize they are people. This is my first indication things are really serious. Not wanting to watch people die, we leave and head for the hotel.

Streets are crowded with people rubbing shoulder to shoulder, but we make our way north. Emergency vehicles are making their way toward the Towers, but they must move slowly because the streets are crowded. People are running to see the Towers, but we continue north. Cell phones will not work. Phone booths have lines of people. We hear that airliners have crashed the Towers. A few minutes later, World Trade Center Two plunges to the ground.

I was ready to die and meet God, but I thank Him that He spared my life. I was never afraid, and I was ready for death because I had prayed one simple prayer. I pray that you will make yourself ready to meet God. Those who did not get out had less than an hour to prepare to meet Him. Some had even less time.

Believe in God's goodness. Believe that He's looking out for you. You are valuable and precious to Him.

Chapter 4

KNOWING WHO YOU ARE

We love the land of Israel and have taken several trips there over the years. Upon boarding El Al Airlines, the official Israeli airline, it's important to know who you are and to be prepared to answer questions regarding your purpose of travel to Israel. El Al Airlines has a reputation for having the toughest, most in-depth security measures in the world, and I can say from experience that we have found that to be true. Not only do the airline employees hand-search every suitcase and bag that you bring on board the plane, but their relentless interrogation by security personnel is unsurpassed. They are stern and direct as they begin asking, "Who are you?" Never batting an eye, they inquire, "Why are you coming to Israel? What is your purpose for being there?" They are looking for any inconsistency in your story, sometimes asking the same question in a different form. Other security personnel are separately asking all members of your party the same questions and taking notes on their responses. After you think you're done with their questions, the second round of inquisition begins by another security guard. As the guards compare notes about each of your responses, they determine if you are a threat to their national security. That can be a little intimidating. In the same way, in your Christian walk you better know who you are and why you are here, because the truth *will* come out! The pressure is being increased and personal identification with Jesus is a necessity.

YOU ARE SEATED WITH CHRIST

Our identity is the core of who we are. Not only is identification based on someone's name, address, and social security number, but it's also about who we perceive ourselves to be. The way we live is related to the innermost thoughts and beliefs that we treasure and hold onto. You will always pull toward those thoughts and beliefs. If you're a Christian but you still think you're a loser and a failure, you will go out losing and failing. If your core belief and mode of thinking is depression, you will be a depressed person. If your core system of thinking and believing is rooted in past sins, you will always live underneath that lid. Winning the battle against the fear of terror requires knowing who you are. Your identity must be with Jesus. He first identified with us when He came from Heaven and took upon Himself human flesh and lived as a man on this earth.

But at the cross is where identification has its greatest revelation. It was there that Jesus took our burden, our sin, and our weaknesses. He did it so that God's punishment that fell upon Him would completely satisfy the claims of justice. Every bit of our weakness, torment, and depression were taken at the cross. After He was resurrected, He identified with us so that now He is able to give us the power to become the sons of God. We identify with His victory, His triumph, and His overcoming ability. Then why should we live a fearful, cowardly life when we're told that "...as He is, so are we in this world" (1 John 4:17)? From First John 4:4, we know that we are of God and have overcome the spirits of antichrist because "greater is He that is in you than he that is in the world" (1 John 4:4 KJV).

Some people think their identity with Christ is something that is going to happen once they die and go to Heaven. They know they're forgiven and saved, but they don't grasp the need to know who they are in this life. If you don't know who you are, then you can't walk in the fullness of what God has for you. It takes faith in the grace of God for us to be identified with Christ.

When our children were small, it seemed that their shoes became too tight about every six months. They grew so fast! But they never had to talk us into giving them shoes that fit. New shoes were given because of a need that our children couldn't meet on their own. As loving parents, we took on the responsibility to provide for our children's needs. They never had to earn what they needed. That's grace, and grace is motivated by love. When we were dead in our sins, God chose to make us alive in Him. He has willingly provided this abundant grace by seating us with Christ in the heavenly place (see Eph. 2:6). We could have never earned that position, nor did we deserve it.

Unfortunately, many Christians don't seem to be aware of this place in Christ. They love God, and they say, "Well, I got saved, and I'm trying to live a victorious life." But when you were born-again, your legal record in the heavenlies changed. You were *made* an overcomer. You were *made* the righteousness of God. When I married Sharon, she went from being a Swift (her maiden name) to a Daugherty. Legally, she was now part of the Daugherty family. When people asked her after we were married, "Who are you?" she never said, "I'm trying to be Sharon Daugherty." No, she didn't have to *try* to be her new identity any more than you have to *try* to be an overcoming Christian. That's just who you are.

Many people who began in the Spirit are trying to complete their life in the works of the flesh, and that's always going to be a defeated battle. It's time to become who God says you are. Although identity theft may be an ongoing problem for some in this world, you don't have to let the devil steal the image that God has placed inside of you. You are more than a conqueror through Christ Jesus (see Rom. 8:37).

YOU ARE A NEW CREATION

The caterpillar's transformation into a butterfly is probably the best visual from nature that explains what takes place at salvation. Caterpillars have a bad reputation for destroying crops and wreaking havoc on the agriculture industry. They look wiggly and furry—harmless looking on the outside—but their appetite is their downfall. It's like a person who is not saved. But through the miraculous metamorphosis that takes place in those caterpillars, they are changed into one of God's most beautiful creatures—the butterfly. Graceful and unassuming, they don't destroy crops. They feed on the nectar of flowers, never harming the beauty of the plant. That reminds me of a sinner saved by grace.

In Second Corinthians 5:17, we find our new identity: "Therefore, if anyone is in Christ, he is a new creation; old things have passed away; behold, all things have become new."

In our hearts, we've been made brand new. A heart of stone has been taken out and a new heart has been put into us. It is a beautiful transformation that takes place inside of us. Many people have the mistaken theological belief that a person is part devil and part God. But when you were born again, God put His nature on the inside of your spirit. Second Corinthians 5:18 says, "Now all things are of God."

Why do Christians still do wrong things? There are two reasons: 1) our mind has not been renewed sufficiently compared to what's happened on the inside of our spirit; or 2) our body has not been surrendered and submitted to who Christ is in us. We are a spirit, we have a soul, and we live in a body. If you get your heart re-born (spirit) and your mind renewed (soul) to who you are in Christ, then it's two to one in your favor. If you're born again but your mind is not renewed and your body is uncontrolled, then it's two to one on the other side. That's where many people's minds and bodies will rule and do wrong things even though their hearts have truly been saved and born again. If you'll feed your spirit, renew your mind, and submit your body to God, then you will live the overcoming life that He intended for you.

YOU ARE A MINISTER

Everyone who is born again is called into the ministry, that is, the ministry of reconciliation. Some are called to stand in a pulpit as pastors, teachers, evangelists, and apostles, but all of us are called to bring people together with God, just as someone did for you. If there's a difference that has separated two people, a reconciler helps them to remove or forgive that difference between them. I hope you haven't forgotten how someone became that reconciler between you and God, presenting the gospel to you in a way that you could understand it. They became a bridge to bring light to your dark world.

As believers, we're all in the bridge-building business. People have sin in their lives, and God is holy. There's a huge chasm that separates them, but the cross is that bridge that connects the two. You and I are the ones who show others those beams lying across the gorge, telling them how God was in Christ "reconciling the world to Himself, not imputing their trespasses to them" (2 Cor. 5:19). God is not mad at sinners; He loves them. But people in the world don't know that. It is our job to tell them the Good News that Jesus died so that they could become children of God. Our lives reflect the One we serve because we are ministers of His message to a lost world. You are a minister.

YOU ARE AN AMBASSADOR

An ambassador assigned to an embassy in a foreign nation is the main source of communication between their homeland and the other nation. People who want to gain access into a country must go through the embassy to get approval. When they finally get approval, their passport is stamped, which allows them entry into the other nation. As a born-again Christian, you are now an ambassador for Christ, and you have a job to do. Second Corinthians 5:20 says that "we are ambassadors for Christ, as though God were pleading through us: we implore you on Christ's behalf, be reconciled to God." The leader of our kingdom is beseeching us to tell the world: "Come to Jesus!" We're to be stamping passports for Heaven while we're here. It's a prestigious job in the Kingdom, and the angels rejoice over every one who confirms their reservations.

Embassies are usually located in the capital city of the foreign country. If you step inside your nation's embassy, it will remind you of your own country even though it's located far from home. The architecture, food, and décor are just like you'd find if you were at home. In our own nation, we have embassies in Washington, DC for every nation with which we have diplomatic ties. As you enter each building, you can get a touch of the flavor from each country. An embassy is also the safest place to be if there is unrest in the foreign country. The ambassador is in direct communication with his or her country's State Department who can advise them of any rescue efforts and plans to protect its citizens. It becomes a refuge for their citizens. As an ambassador in God's kingdom, however, you carry your embassy with you. Not only do you have safety as you live in the presence of God and His Kingdom boundaries, but you are the lifeline to a desperate and dying world. When people are in trouble, they will come to you to help them get to safety. Don't shirk your responsibility in this important occupation.

CHRIST IS IN YOU

People may have put labels on you in the past, saying that you're weak, that you don't have the qualifications, that you're a failure, or that you'll never amount to anything. I want to crush that image with the truth of the Word of God. First John 4:4 says, "You are of God, little children, and you have overcome them [the spirits of antichrist] because greater is He that is in you than he that is in the world." When you were born again, Christ came to live in you and you in Him. Colossians 1:27 says, "Christ in you, the hope of glory." That's present tense—He's here, alive, living on the inside of you right now. His spirit is in your spirit because you are joined to the Lord (see 1 Cor. 6:17).

WILL THE "REAL YOU" PLEASE KEEP STANDING?

If people choose, they can live life without allowing Jesus to come into their lives and change them. But they'll have to carry all of their burdens, their failures, and their sins, and they will never be done paying for them. Or they can recognize that Jesus died on the cross to save them and live life on the other side of the cross, believing that Jesus took their sin, failures, and burdens for them.

Jesus made a comparison between a wise and foolish person in Matthew 7. He told about a storm that came to two different houses. The winds beat against each dwelling. As a result, one house stood and one fell. The difference between the two houses was their foundation. The dwelling that stood had been built upon a rock, and the one that fell was built upon sand (see Matt. 7:24-27). Many people stop there and figure that means that if you build on Jesus, the Rock, then your house won't fall. That's good, but there's more that Jesus was saying through that story.

If you study the story, you will find that both of the men *heard* the Lord's commands, but only one of them (the wise man) *did* what He said. That was the difference. The house that stood was built by the wise man who *heard* and *did* what

Jesus said. James wrote that if a Christian only hears the Word of God but doesn't do what it says, he or she is self-deceived. It is the doer of the Word of God who will be blessed with experiencing God's promises (see James 1:22-25). This explains why some Christians see God work miraculously in their lives and other Christians live in defeat, destruction, and depression.

I believe that you're like that wise man and that you will choose to walk in the truth of who you are so that you can stand strong. Remember who you are, and continue to walk in that reality. Here's a recap:

You are seated with Christ in heavenly places (see Eph. 2:6).

You are a new creation (see 2 Cor. 5:17).

You are a minister of reconciliation (see 2 Cor. 5:18).

You are an ambassador for Christ—a Christ-bearer (see 2 Cor. 5:20).

Christ is in you (see Col. 1:27).

You become wise by being a doer of the Word of God, not a hearer only (see Matt. 7:24-27; James 1:22-25).

Our identity is no longer in who we *were*; it's in who we are *now* in Jesus Christ. Understanding who you really are will put a confidence in you that will enable you to reach for your destiny. If the devil begins accusing you about your past or threatening to expose who you *were*, the "real you" can confidently say, "The greater one lives in me!" No longer are you a slave to your former way of life. You are now in Him. That's who you really are.

Chapter 5

GOD IS ON YOUR SIDE

On September 12, 2001, one day after the infamous terror attacks on the United States of America, history was made. For the first time since it was signed in 1949, Article 5 of the North Atlantic Treaty went into effect. This article states: "The Parties agree that an armed attack against one or more of them in Europe or North America shall be considered an attack against them all."[1] By this alliance, they are bound to defend any member country that is attacked, using force when necessary. The war on terror began. Our allies became as committed to the cause as if their country had been attacked.

But we have something that is more powerful than the NATO agreement. It's the covenant that we have through our Lord Jesus Christ. Fear has no place in our lives when we know that we're right with God through faith in what Jesus did. It is stopped and driven back from us. Though we may be weak, we have a strong elder brother (Jesus Christ), and by faith in His righteousness (or right standing), we have become allies with God. An attack against you is an attack against God Himself. Now, there's an alliance! Paul, the apostle, prayed that the eyes of our understanding would be opened so that we could see the power that we've been given in Christ over the enemy (see

Eph. 1:17-23). When we as a Church get the same revelation that Peter did concerning who Jesus is, then, as Jesus said, "The gates of Hades *shall not* prevail against [us]" (Matt. 16:18).

GROUNDED IN RIGHTEOUSNESS

To understand how the power of God is released in our lives through our faith in Jesus Christ, we have to be grounded in our right-standing with God. It's easy to understand that Jesus is righteous (or in right-standing) with God. He is the Son of God, and He was obedient to the cross. However, some Christians have struggled with accepting that He paid the price on the cross to make us righteous. Through faith in what Jesus has done for us, we become righteous before God. Second Corinthians 5:21 says, "For He made Him who knew no sin to be sin for us, that we might become the righteousness of God in Him."

Deep inside of all people throughout history is a need to be right within themselves. If you study the ancient civilizations of the world (the Sumerians, Babylonians, Egyptians, Assyrians, Greeks, Romans, Aztecs, Incas, or Mayas), you will find that they all had some symbol or emblem that represented an attempt to appease what they would call the "gods." The pyramids of Egypt and those huge Central American and Mexican pyramids were used for human sacrifices. They would try to appease the gods through the blood of their sons and daughters, and when they felt that the gods were happy with them, then their crops would grow and life would be well with them. All civilizations have had attempts at this. These same efforts are evident in any tribal group, whether it's in South America, Africa, or the islands of the Pacific.

Guilt and condemnation are what drive fear, inferiority, and anxiety in many people. Humankind craves to be freed from guilt and to have a sense of rightness with God. When people do not understand what the Bible says concerning righteousness, they make many attempts on their own to pay for their sins. Once we know that God did it through His own Son, then we begin to believe in His work rather than in our works. This message is the central theme of the whole Bible. Adam and Eve had right-standing with God in the garden, but they lost it. The story of the Bible is how humankind got it ("right-standing") back through Jesus Christ and how He gave His righteousness to us.

RIGHTEOUS BY *FAITH*

Many years ago I was preaching a series of meetings in a church, and the Lord dealt with me to preach on righteousness every night that week. I didn't know it at the time, but there was a good reason. In this small church, there was a man in the front row who was a Sunday school teacher, chief elder in the church, and he had been there many years. He was highly respected in the church and was a man of God. I respected him, too. But he did not accept the teaching about righteousness. He did not agree with it, and he just didn't like it. He had been stuck on the Scriptures "There is none righteous, no, not one" (Rom. 3:10) and "...All our righteousnesses are like filthy rags..." (Isa. 64:6).

As I was preaching on this, and from his seat on the front row, he was verbally negating everything I said. As I would read a Scripture about our being made righteous, he'd let me know he didn't agree with it by shaking his head in disagreement or flatly saying, "No, no, no." This went on for three nights. Every night I pleaded with the Lord, "Do I have to go back again and preach this?" It got to the point where everybody in the congregation was watching us during the services. I would say something from the pulpit, and they'd look at this brother in the Lord to see how he would respond. I never said anything negative about it, but I was having a terrible time preaching in that place. By the fourth night of that teaching, however, something changed. I was preaching that you are righteous *by faith* in what Jesus Christ did. Finally, the revelation hit him. He said out loud, "Praise God! I've got it! It's by faith!" And I was thinking, *Praise God, you got it!*

If people feel condemned, unworthy, and unrighteous, then their faith can't rise to receive the healing or deliverance that they need. Romans 8:1 says, "There is therefore now no condemnation to those who are in Christ Jesus, who do not walk according to the flesh, but according to the Spirit." We are no longer condemned for our past because we have, by faith, received God's gift of righteousness. We aren't righteous because we've done the right things; we want to do right things because we *are* righteous.

When you understand that righteousness has been given to you as a gift through your belief in the cleansing blood of Jesus Christ, you don't want to go back into living in sin. You've been set free from sin's control, and now Jesus Christ is in you enabling you to do the right thing and resist the temptation of sin. You now have a desire to walk in "paths of righteousness" (see Ps. 23:3). It's like this: Why would someone who has taken a shower and is clean and wearing clean clothes want to go jump into a mud puddle and get dirty? You not only want to do the right thing, but now you have the power to do it.

YOUR RIGHTEOUSNESS IS OF HIM

When you realize that you are righteous through faith in Jesus because "Him who knew no sin He made to be sin on our behalf; that we might be made the righteousness of God in Him," (2 Cor. 5:21 ASV), you now have confidence in prayer. God has given us promises throughout the Bible that we can pray and know that God will answer us. In James Moffatt's recent translation of the Bible, James 5:16 reads, "The prayers of the righteous have a powerful effect." Now when you pray according to His Word, which is His will, you have confidence that God hears and answers your prayers (see 1 John 5:14-15).

Because our righteousness is based on our faith in what the Lord has given us, we have promises from the Word of God that we can now stand on and believe that He will deliver us from evil. Your inheritance includes protection from your enemies. Isaiah 54:17 declares:

"No weapon formed against you shall prosper, and every tongue which rises against you in judgment you shall condemn. This is the heritage of the servants of the Lord, and their righteousness is from Me," says the Lord.

For any weapon that the enemy has fashioned against us— could be a car bomb, a missile, a knife, a gun, or a deadly disease—we need to say what the Word of God says about it: "Lord, I thank You that no weapon formed against me shall prosper."

Isaiah 54:17 became very real to us as we held monthly crusades in St. Petersburg, Russia, in the early 1990s. We began in December 1991, just as the Cold War was ending, which opened the door for ministries to more openly take the gospel into Russia. Many Russians traveled for miles through all types of weather and travel conditions to reach the crusades. However, not everyone welcomed us with open arms. There was a group of people that got together and plotted to stop us by picketing and shouting at the people who were attending the crusades. It was important for their harassment of the people to stop in order for the people to come and receive salvation. We prayed, "Lord, thank You that You're going to shut their mouths and You're going to deal with it." God worked it out. The group's antics drew the media's attention, giving us a little more publicity. More people became curious and came to see what was going on at the SKK convention center. It was standing-room-only as people flooded that place to see the power of God move. What the devil had meant for harm, God turned around for His good.

In the same set of meetings in Russia, a guy in a trench coat was reaching up to me on the stage as if he wanted to shake my hand. I started to bend over to shake hands, and just as I did, the Holy Spirit said, "Don't do it!" and I jerked back. The man suddenly threw open his jacket and pulled out a sign with something written in Russian. He started screaming at the crowd in Russian and pointing at me. Evidently, he had planned to pull me off that stage. Here I was in another country, trying to spread the love of God. I didn't intentionally want to offend someone who appeared to be kind, but when I heard those words from the Holy Spirit, that settled the issue. Sometimes you may have to make quick decisions that to others might seem rude or insensitive. When you hear from the Spirit of God, however, you are responsible to obey Him before man. He is the Revealer of truth, and He will guide you in the right path.

What the man had not counted on when he planned his attack was that on the front row were all the Russian grandmothers—the *babushkas* as they are called. They had gotten saved, and many of them had prayed and held on to their faith all through the years of communism. As this guy started screaming at the audience, all of these ladies came and attacked him right there in front of the whole crowd. They were kicking, biting, scratching, and punching this guy. They grabbed him and carried him out of the building. At that point we had compassion on him and were praying, "Lord, deliver him from the *babushkas!*"

THE GREAT EXCHANGE

So how does righteousness play a part in combating fear and terror? According to Isaiah 54:14, "In righteousness you shall be established; you shall be far from oppression, for you shall not fear; and from terror, for it shall not come near you." *Established* means that you've meditated on it and you're settled in it. The more established you are in your righteousness, the further fear, torment, and oppression will be from you. I'm not talking about self-righteousness, which is based on people's attempts to be righteous in their own self-efforts. That is a never-ending battle and will only keep you defeated. What I'm referring to is the *gift of righteousness* that comes through faith in Jesus Christ. Romans 5:17 says, "For if by the one man's offense death reigned through the one [Adam], much more those who receive abundance of grace and of the gift of righteousness will reign in life through the One, Jesus Christ."

Jesus was made to be our sin so that we could receive this gift from God. That's what the cross was all about. Many people died on crosses at the time that Jesus was here on the earth, but He was the Son of the living God. He was righteous and holy. He not only bore our sin but He bore God's wrath for sin as well. Jesus took the blows that should have fallen on you and me. We should have died. We should have been separated from God and experienced that judgment. But Jesus, because of His great love, took our place. There is no greater love story. There never has been; there never will be. This was the great exchange.

Jesus took the worst in us to give us the best in Him. Maybe you were a liar, a cheat, or an abuser, and the enemy keeps pointing back at what you did. If you live in that condemnation, you will keep repeating that sin. It's just like a baseball player who misses a ground ball and then keeps thinking about his mistake. The next time a ball comes, he's going to miss it again until he "shakes it off," letting the past be the past. If you've repented, you have to forget what happened and go on.

But what if you mess up now? First John 2:1 says that we still have an advocate at the right hand of the Father, Jesus Christ, the righteous One. When you confess and repent of that sin, First John 1:9 says, "...He is faithful and just to forgive us our sins and to cleanse us from all unrighteousness." If you are cleansed from all unrighteousness by confessing your sins, what does that leave you? It leaves you righteous, completely forgiven, and free to boldly carry out God's will in the earth.

KEEP ON KEEPING ON

God has set us on a path to finish the work that He started. We can't look back or step back in fear. We have to finish our course. Hebrews 12:1 tells us to "lay aside every weight, and the sin which so easily ensnares us." If you've strayed from the path somewhere along the way, get back up. The only way that you can lose this race is if you quit.

I ran track in junior high and remember how hard it was to finish that last stretch. I wasn't very fast, but I ran what they called the "quarter mile" back then—one time around the track. During one particular meet, while I was in the starting blocks getting ready to run, I heard a familiar voice yelling for me in the stands, "Come on, Billy Joe!" It was my dad up there cheering me on. At that age, I didn't want to stand out from my peers or have any attention drawn to myself. I was a little embarrassed by how he was carrying on. About that time, the gun fired to signal that the race had begun, so I took off running as fast as I could.

We went down the first curve and all the way down the back stretch. As I came around the final curve, the last 110 yards, I began to hear my dad's voice: "Come on, Billy Joe! Come on, Billy Joe! Come on, Billy Joe!" That voice seemed closer than it should have been. As I looked to my left, there was my dad. He was inside the running track, matching me step for step all the way to the finish line. He cheered as he ran, "Come on, Billy Joe!" It made a great impression on me. I'll never forget it.

Many years later, as I reflected on what my dad had done for me on the track that day, I thought of Jesus. Jesus came out of the grandstands of Heaven, came to this earth, and got up on the cross for you and me. He knows our weaknesses and what we can't do on our own. But through His resurrection, He's running beside us, matching us step for step along the way, cheering us on, "Come on! You can make it! I'm with you! You have My strength, My ability, My power! Now run with all your might!"

There's no way that you can run this race on your own. You need God's help to make it. Hebrews 12:2 says that Jesus went before us, finished His course, and then sat down at the end of His race. That's why we keep our focus on Him, "the author and finisher of our faith" (Heb. 12:2). He's been where you are, fought what you fight, and won in the end. He's seated at the Father's right hand, cheering you on. With God on your side, you cannot lose.

ENDNOTE

1. "The North Atlantic Treaty," April 4, 1948, Article 5, *NATO Official Text On-line Library,* http://www.nato.int/docu/basictxt/Treaty.htm (accessed 22 March 2007).

Chapter 6

FREEDOM FROM FEAR

Springtime in Oklahoma is beautiful! The birds are trying to build nests wherever they can. The beautiful Bradford pear trees line the streets of Tulsa, bright white with blooms. And many of the lawns have what looks like a groundcover of precious yellow flowers. The dandelions are back! We could mow over them, but in a day or two, they'd pop up with their bright yellow shoots and bring more of their friends with them. Their heads are filled with seeds that will be scattered over the whole yard with the lightest breeze, ensuring that we'll have more to deal with next year, too.

This same analogy holds true in the lives of people. If people don't act quickly and confront their issues, they'll have a fuzzy head of distress on them which causes more problems than the pesky yellow flowers (life's little annoyances). Weeds choke out the good life of the plants around them. They proudly take over, pushing out the plants or grass that you want and replacing it with themselves. Who needs them? Who wants them? There are two ways to deal with them. Number one: Hire a lawn company to spray herbicide on them. That's not a bad idea. Number two: Pull them out at the roots, which will forever deal with the individual weeds. It's a big job, but it's an effective way to make sure you're not dealing with the same problem over and over again.

Think of fear as a weed in your garden of life. It has been trying to suffocate your God-ordained purpose and convince you that there's no way out, that life will always be like this. Left to itself, fear will force you into slavery—in your thoughts and your actions. It's time to deal with it head-on. Today is your day to pull out fear by the roots.

THE ROOT OF FEAR

People try to get fear out of their lives through various gimmicks. They try to get over things and deal with them. That's fine for some people, but when you're ready to deal with the root cause of fear and yank it out of your life—no longer just putting up with it and accommodating it—then you have to go to the Word of God to find the answer. Hebrews 2:14-15 tells us that "through death He [Jesus] might destroy him who had the power of death, that is, the devil, and release those who through fear of death were all their lifetime subject to bondage."

There it is: The root of fear is the fear of death. Why does the fear of death have such power over people? They dread the impending judgment that they know follows in the hereafter. Life on this planet will come to an end, and then people will come face-to-face with God. Hebrews 12:29 says that our God is a consuming fire. That's a reality. Up until the cross, the devil had the power of death. He ruled man with an iron fist because of the curse of sin from the fall of Adam. He still rules millions of people who don't know the truth. First Corinthians 15:56

says, "The sting of death is sin, and the strength of sin is the law." Death stings because of sin. Sin pays big dividends. It's called death (see Rom. 6:23). That's death in every way—physical, spiritual, eternal.

The law was given to humanity to show us our need for a Savior. Humankind has tried to keep all God's laws but to no avail. It's futile. No matter how good you might think you are, you're not good enough. You can't do it on your own. Facing judgment on our own merits in front of a holy God is a horrifying thought. People may on the surface say they don't believe in God, but when it comes right down to it, their souls know better. They're pushing down the "what if" thought that nags them: *What if there is a God? What if there is a judgment for what I've done?* It causes fear and anxiety as they realize that they will die one day. That's because there is one fear that they have neglected to embrace—the fear of the Lord.

THE FEAR OF THE LORD

I want to caution you about one fear that is too often neglected but is absolutely necessary. My advice to you is to find it at all costs. This fear is valid and warranted. It will keep you on the path of life, always pulling you away from the world's ways of destruction. Taking it too lightly can result in devastating consequences that none of us are able to bear. Isaiah 8:13 tells us about this fear: "The Lord of hosts, Him you shall hallow; let Him be your fear, and let Him be your dread."

The fear of the Lord is not to be confused with internal or external fears that cause torment. On the contrary, it is life-giving and full of expectation toward the will of God. It does not mean being afraid that God might decide to hurt you. God loves you, but He has established boundaries and spiritual laws. If someone goes beyond those, they will have trouble. The fear of the Lord is the respect and honor that we give Him by keeping His commandments. If you have any wisdom, you'll keep the fear of the Lord. Psalms 111:10 calls it "the beginning of wisdom."

When we honor God, we want to obey Him and follow after His ways. Proverbs 19:23 says that the fear of the Lord "leads to life, and he who has it will abide in satisfaction; he will not be visited with evil." This fear is about submitting to God, whatever it takes. The honor for God that I'm talking about is the realization that He's God and that we're not. Some people call that having a "healthy respect" for God, but they still do what they want. If you have the true fear of the Lord, however, you will depart from (or get away from) evil (see Prov. 16:6). You won't put up with a little bit of it, just like you would not put up with having a snake coiled around your feet while you go to sleep. That's foolishness!

In our democratic society, we have been allowed to voice our opinions openly about anybody or anything without retribution from authorities. It's been our "right" to say what we want about leaders and others in authority. That philosophy has caused some confusion about God's position of authority. Allow me to explain. God is not *a* king; He is *the* King. God is not *a* president; He is *the* One who presides over the ultimate destiny of humanity and all that we know in the universe. Humanity didn't just happen to appear on the earth by some fluke of nature; God pre-ordained and planned our existence. He is the Creator God and is incomparable. God is God all by Himself. He is the absolute ultimate authority. We cannot have a casual attitude about God. God is love, but God is just. He will judge all things. He will not be mocked or stopped without demonstrating His almighty power.

Those who have experienced the tangible presence of the Lord when revival has hit the Church can attest to the fire that accompanies His presence. One such incident comes from the Argentine Revival in 1950. On Christmas Day that year in the middle of the Chaco jungle, Alexander and his friends were set on fire by the Spirit of God. In the book *Secrets of the Argentine Revival*, Dr. R. Edward Miller recounts Alexander's story:

> Alexander, the wayward, rebellious son of the pastor who was the ring leader of a gang of mischief-makers, came to the church with the express purpose of disturbing the meeting. He was standing at the church door with his cronies making fun of the service. In a half-drunken state, he felt himself drawn irresistibly forward by a great wave of fire. Nearing the altar, he gave a great cry and suddenly threw himself down on the floor. His laughter had turned into great mournful cries for mercy and he began to weep uncontrollably. His rebellious companions, who had followed him into the church, turned and tried to escape, but it was too late. One-by-one they all dropped to the floor crying out as if their souls were already in hell.

Those men repented and turned to the Lord because they experienced the fear of the Lord that resulted in their salvation.

THE FEAR-REMOVER

We now know that man's greatest fear is the fear of death and judgment because of sin. Going back to Hebrews 2:14 in the Amplified Bible, we read what Jesus' death meant for our sentence: "that by [going through] death He [Jesus] might bring to nought and make of no effect him who had the power of death—that is, the devil." The cross settled the issue. Satan lost power over us and our judgment. It was at that time that our eternal address changed from hell to Heaven.

Tommy Barnett pastors a church in Phoenix, Arizona, and he and his son, Matthew, founded the Los Angeles Dream Center. Many years ago he lived in Davenport, Iowa, where a group began to push pornography in all of the convenience stores. He led a campaign of ministers and Christians to stand up against it and to get it removed from those places. His exposing of the truth cut into the group's revenue, so they sent people to try to kill him. He was interviewed on one of the network stations on national news at the time and was asked, "Aren't you afraid of being killed?" He looked right into the camera, laughed, and said, "You can't scare a Christian with Heaven."[2] Tommy knew the power of the cross. He walked in that revelation.

So why are so many Christians still walking in fear? Why does terror grip them when they hear a negative doctor's report? It's because they're missing the motive behind the cross. Romans 5:7 says that there's a possibility that a man might give up his life for someone he esteems, someone who is thought to be a good man. That would be noble, wouldn't it? "But God demonstrates His own love toward us, in that while we were still sinners, Christ died for us" (Rom. 5:8). God did what no one would or could do. When Jesus gave His life for us, we were completely lost. There was no hope whatsoever for us. He took a huge risk to give His only Son for an ungodly bunch of people. This is true love. Real love is not a gushy, emotional, lustful thing. Love is sacrifice.

When you truly take in that kind of love, then fear is out the window. *How* you will die—which is an unknown for everyone on this planet—has no bearing on you because His love swallows that fear too. You know that since He loves you as much as He does, He has that covered for you. Then First John 4:18 makes sense to you: "There is no fear in love, but perfect loves casts out fear." It has no power. It is kicked out. There is *no fear* in love. His love removes the fear of death and of judgment. Once we know that He gave His one and only Son for us and canceled our sins, we can receive His forgiveness. We have the witness of His Spirit inside of our hearts. We have the love of God down inside of us and the absolute knowledge that at the judgment we will be declared not guilty. Fear of terror has no more power over us. We're not afraid of terrorists abroad. We're not afraid of getting on an airplane or going someplace. We're not afraid of the dark, and we're not afraid of going home by ourselves. We're not scared of any threat against our lives. God's love will swallow our fears and allow us to carry on with our lives without interruption.

As we study the Word of God, we realize that God has given His promise to every Christian and a long life if they believe and walk in His commands. Psalm 90:10 says that we should live to at least seventy years old, or eighty *if we are strong.* This can be even longer as we believe that He still has purposes for us to accomplish and as we break free from fear's grip of control and intimidation.

BREAKING THE CONTROL OF FEAR

People who are particularly prone to fear's control are those who've grown up in abusive environments. Abusers control their victims by fear. A lady in our church named Cheryl grew up in a home that was abusive in every way—verbally, physically, sexually, and emotionally. The abuse was so bad that the law enforcement authorities in every city they lived in documented it. Fear of her father and mother ruled their household. Her parents did allow her to ride the bus to churches. Cheryl was born again through a church's bus ministry and received some nurture and care through the church that she lacked at home. Dirty and smelly, she remembers being hugged and treated with care. She felt the unconditional love of God through the church people. It was something she would never forget.

As a teenager, she left her family and later married, only to be abandoned by her husband when she was pregnant with their child. She began to look for a church to attend and came to ours. Week by week, she received the revelation of God's love for her and the revelation of who she was in Christ. Her life was restored, and she grew in her understanding that God needed her life to help others. The love of God had replaced the fear of rejection and control that she had lived under. But that love was put to a test. She wrote a minibook to help other women who had experienced similar abuse. However, when *Victory Over Abuse*[3] was first released, her father got a copy of the book and was enraged. He said that everything in the book was a lie. Through a family member she was warned that he threatened to kill her and her son during the Christmas holiday that year.

Frightened, Cheryl asked Sharon to pray for her. They agreed in prayer with the promises of God's Word that her father could not harm her or her son. She then decided to stay with another single parent mom until she felt that it was safe to go back home. A couple of days into her stay, she realized that not only did she not know when he planned to show up at her house, but she also didn't know how long this threat could last. She recalled the love that God had for her. It strengthened her to go back home and face the fear. She felt that she needed to make contact with her dad and made arrangements for her and a friend to meet him at a neutral location. He agreed to it. By the time she had sat down across from him at the restaurant that day, she had settled the fear issue in herself. She told him, "I'm not afraid of you. I have documentation to back up everything that I've said in the book. I have gone on with my life, and I've prayed for your salvation. I forgive you, and I'll never be afraid of you ever again." He never attempted to make contact with her again.

He died later and never apologized to her for what he had put her and her brothers and sisters through as children. Although her father was unable to show her appropriate love while on this earth, her heavenly Father's love has far exceeded anything she could have imagined. Cheryl now works in our ministry in the television department and accompanies us on overseas crusade trips. She has shared her testimony in many nations and has had her book transcribed into other languages. Everywhere we go, people identify with her story. Altar calls are filled with others who have been through abuse and desire freedom and victory. What the devil intended for evil, God has turned for good. Cheryl has led many to Jesus Christ and brought His healing power to many lives. Fear has been removed because Cheryl received and choose to live in the love of God.

HIS LOVE WILL GUIDE YOU

There are situations where people have depended upon their natural ability to discern when to avoid dangerous situations. Now that you know the love of God, you must shift gears to trust in His love to guide you instead. Proverbs 3:5-6 says it best: "Trust in the LORD with all your heart, and lean not on your own understanding; in all your ways acknowledge Him, and He shall direct your paths."

You must know it deep down in your spirit, "God loves me. If God loves me, He is going to guide me. He's going to direct my steps." God's Holy Spirit comes to live inside of us when we are born again. He leads and guides us in our spirits if we listen to His promptings. John 16:13 says, "Yet when that one I have spoken to you about comes—the Spirit of truth—He will guide you into everything that is true... he will inform you about what is to come" (Phillips). Because He loves you, He will direct you away from evil. He's in you to help you walk out God's plans and purposes, but you must listen to His thoughts and obey Him. He may direct you to leave a restaurant and go to a different one. Or He may lead you to change from one flight to another. There could also be what appears to be a delay in your scheduled plans or a re-routing of a trip. Because your steps are ordered of the Lord, trust Him to take you where He intends you to be when He intends for you to be there.

With God's love navigating your life, you can be in what may be a hostile environment for others, but for you it is peaceful and refreshing. Sharon and I experienced that several years ago when we visited Israel. We arrived a couple of days after terrorists had bombed a disco in Tel Aviv. A bunch of Russian and Ukrainian young people were killed in that incident. Our family walked down the middle of the street near where the bombings had occurred and realized that the suicide bombers had been near that location just days before. But we felt no fear whatsoever.

We visited Bethlehem, which was under Palestinian rule at the time. Tensions between the Arabs and Israelis were especially high because the Israelis had entered at various times but were not occupying at the moment. Israeli tanks and armored vehicles surrounded the city. At the checkpoint, we had to change buses from an Israeli bus to an Arab bus, but once again, we felt no fear of being in the area. Bethlehem is where the Church of the Nativity is located, which is the historical place where they say Jesus was born. We wanted to see it, so we were escorted to the church by PLO (Palestinian Liberation Organization) soldiers. Knowing that we were in the perfect will of God removed all fear of what could happen while we were there. It wasn't even an issue.

We have known and we have believed the love that God has for us. Therefore, anthrax, nuclear weapons, and terrorists do not cause us to fear. Neither does tomorrow or the next day or the day after that. Now that we know the power of His love to transform us, it's time for us pass it on.

ENDNOTES

1. R. Edward Miller, *Secrets of the Argentine Revival* (Fairburn, GA: Peniel Publications, 1999), 55.

2. Tommy Barnett, interview.

3. Lynn, Cheryl. *Victory Over Abuse* (Tulsa, OK: Cheryl Lynn Ministries, Inc., 2004).

Chapter 7

LIVING IN FREEDOM

Second Timothy 3 tells us that there will be perilous times in the last days:

For men will be lovers of themselves, lovers of money, boasters, proud, blasphemers, disobedient to parents, unthankful, unholy, unloving, unforgiving, slanderers, without self-control, brutal, despisers of good, traitors, headstrong, haughty, lovers of pleasure rather than lovers of God (2 Timothy 3:2-4).

That just about sums up where we are in today's society. But we have a different spirit. We no longer have the spirit of this world; we have the spirit of God living in us. From First John 4:16 we learn that "God is love, and he who abides in love abides in God, and God in him."

The faith that you need to stay free of fear will *not* be there when you need it *if you're not walking in love.* Second Timothy 1:7 says that we have not been given a spirit of fear, but of power, love, and a sound mind. You have the Spirit of power. That means that you're in charge. The devil is not in control of you. You have the love of God in you. Evil does not control you. And you have a sound mind. Your thoughts no longer run rampant without control. Fear is not in charge of you when you walk in the love of God.

LEARNING TO LOVE

We are living in a day and a time when we (believers) have what the world needs. They are looking for acceptance and love, craving it from the depths of their souls. While some worship a god who keeps them in constant fear, our God is full of love and mercy. We reflect the God that we serve. The world's perspective of love is, "What's in it for me?" It's all about the big *I*—"I don't love you because you don't make me happy." It's self-centered and has no depth to it. When tough times come, the world's love walks out the door.

We all need a refresher course on what love looks like as it relates to how we act toward other people. The movies can't tell us; the soap operas and talk shows don't have a clue. Love may not be what you think. From First Corinthians 13:4-8, we find the answer:

Love endures long and is patient and kind; love never is envious nor boils over with jealousy, is not boastful or vainglorious, does not display itself haughtily. It is not conceited (arrogant and inflated with pride); it is not rude (unmannerly) and does not act unbecomingly. Love (God's love in us) does not insist on its own rights or its own way, for it is not self-seeking; it is not touchy or fretful or resentful; it takes no account of the evil done to it [it pays no attention to a suffered wrong]. It does not rejoice at injustice and unrighteousness, but rejoices when right and truth prevail. Love bears up under anything and everything that comes, is ever ready to believe the best of every person, its hopes are fadeless under all circumstances, and it endures everything [without weakening]. Love never fails [never fades out or becomes obsolete or comes to an end] (AMP).

So if people threaten us, we're going to love them back. If they attack us, we're going to respond with love. If they speak against us or plot against us, we're going to love them. I'm not talking about letting someone abuse you and just taking it. You have to protect yourself and family members from people who threaten or intend to harm you. But love will continue to pray and believe God for a turnaround in that person's life.

Early on in our ministry, we walked through some difficult circumstances with several people, and the Lord told us, "You just walk in love. You just do the right thing, and I will bring you through." And He always did. Why did those things happen to us? I don't know. We may not always be able to explain all the reasons that some things happen, but we can believe that God can turn it around if we'll do what's right. Maturing in your love walk is a process. It doesn't just automatically happen at the age of 16, 18, or 21. And it doesn't happen just because you've been saved a long time. It happens to the degree that your surrendered heart says, "I choose to love; I choose to forgive." Every one of us has an opportunity on a daily basis to make that choice. When you go the love way, you will never miss.

CLOSE THE DOOR ON STRIFE

We may be speaking the Word of God for protection, believing that we receive His love, and standing on His promises, but if our love walk is not happening, it's an open door to disaster. James 3:16 says: "For where envy and self-seeking exist, confusion and every evil thing are there." The King James Version has another word for *self-seeking* and that's the word *strife*. Strife comes out of self-seeking. Wherever there's strife or quarreling, there's an opportunity for evil. That's why we need to shut the door on quarreling, bitterness, or resentment in our own hearts. I want to encourage you to stay out of strife with the people around you—your spouse, children, parents, co-workers, and neighbors, or the guy on the road, the bank teller, or even the president of the United States! Some people are mad at what the president did or didn't do and become so irate that they can hardly think straight. It's time to let that go so that you can walk in freedom.

Sometimes people say, "Well, I have a right to be angry. I have a right to hold a grudge or hold resentment." Well, you may feel that you have a right. But I want to ask you: Is it worth getting out of the place of divine protection? Forgiving others in spite of what they have done is a sign of mature love. Forgiveness is a choice. In your greatest pain, it is time to forgive. It's not the time to hold a grudge; it's the time to release the offense. When you do that, you have no fear because the awareness of God's presence is with you.

If you've had bitter animosity, ill will, or a wrong feeling in your heart toward some person, this is a warning to you to let go of it. God wants to free you of it. It's time to come to that place of maturity, letting go, and forgiving. It's not worth holding it. Maybe what they did was wrong. If you're over them in authority (as a parent or employer), you're going to have to address the issues. You can do it without hatred and malice. But if it's someone you don't have authority over, rest assured, God will take care of it in His way and His time. Be in right relationship with God so that you can have the confidence that He is working on your behalf.

When Sharon and I first started out in the ministry, we were in our early twenties. The church where we were on staff held a week-long series of meetings with a well-known Bible teacher who had been in the ministry many years. I was young and eager to step into my calling, and I sensed that he would have some good advice if I could just have the opportunity to talk to him. At the end of the meeting, I spotted him in the parking lot as he was walking to his car. I ran up alongside him and kept pace with him and said, "Sir, I have just started out in the ministry. I was just wondering if there was one thing you could tell me that would help me in ministry, what would it be?" Without missing a step, he said, "If you don't get bitter, you'll make it," and he kept walking. I have lived by that advice ever since, not only in ministry but also in everyday life in my personal relationships. As we've chosen to forgive and let go of offense, we have seen God move on our behalf. As we continue to walk in His love, we find that it is one of the greatest weapons that we have against the devil.

Remember, James 3:16 says that where envy and strife (or self-seeking) exist, there is opportunity for evil to work. Strife opens the door for satan to cause trouble, calamity, sickness, and any other form of evil. Years ago a lady in our church who was a strong Christian and who loved the Lord went through a situation where God gave her understanding of this Scripture.

Her husband worked for the newspaper, and every Saturday night he had to work through the night until the wee hours of the next morning. He would come home and sleep a few hours and meet her at church for the 11:00 A.M. service. She taught Sunday school early each Sunday morning and would wait on him to join her for the church service. Many times he overslept, and this began to frustrate her to the point that she had strife toward him. One Sunday, when he had overslept, she was driving home to meet him in their new car, and she had an accident. Of course, her husband was not happy that she had wrecked the new car.

A few days later, she shared that as she was ironing clothes, she asked the Lord, "Why did the accident happen? I have my Bible reading time daily. I pray Psalm 91 over my life, my husband, and my children every day, and I believe I'm in covenant with You, Lord, and that I have Your covenant protection." She said she heard the Lord say within her heart, "Because of strife." Immediately she knew God was showing her the strife she had toward her husband. Strife opened the door to an opportunity where satan could attack her. She immediately repented to God and then to her husband. She knew the call of God was upon their lives for ministry and she had released the timing to God. Not long after this, God began to deal with her husband's heart regarding a change in their lives and obeying the call of God. They became pastors, and God has used their lives to minister to many people.

Love overpowers the enemy. It is a shield that can protect your life. Colossians 3:13-14 says, "bearing with one another, and forgiving one another, if anyone has a complaint against another; even as Christ forgave you, so you also must do. But above all these things put on love, which is the bond of perfection." The Revised Standard Version of verse 14 says, "...[love] binds everything together in perfect harmony."

Nicky Cruz, former New York City gang member, who was converted to Jesus Christ through David Wilkerson's efforts, shares how his life had been filled with strife and hatred. He was raised by parents involved in witchcraft, and they were abusive to him as a child. He left home as a teenager and lived on the streets of New York City. His life was filled with drugs, immorality, and murder. When David Wilkerson heard of these gangs of young people on the streets of New York, he knew he had to reach them with the gospel of Jesus Christ. The love of God led him right into the dark places that they lived. David was threatened, mocked, and rejected, but he pressed through it all and kept going to them because of love.

Nicky said that one day David came up to him again to talk to him about Jesus Christ and how Jesus loved him. Nicky couldn't get those words out of his head, "Jesus loves you." He reached over to grab David so that he could hurt him, and David responded, "You could kill me, Nicky. You could cut me in a thousand pieces and lay them out on the street. But every piece would cry out, Jesus loves you. And you'll never be able to run from that"[1] Nicky tried to stab David several times at that moment, but it was as if David was surrounded by an invisible shield. Nicky became scared for the first time in his life. Every night he tried to lie down and sleep, but he couldn't. All he could think of was David Wilkerson and his words. Finally, Nicky surrendered his life to Jesus Christ and became one of David's first street gang converts that attended Teen Challenge. Nicky has been preaching the gospel for over forty years now.

God's love in you is a powerful weapon that will enable you to stay free from fear in this life. When God guides and you move in His love, there is an invisible shield of protection that no power of darkness can penetrate.

ENDNOTE

1. Nicky Cruz and Jamie Buckingham, *Run Baby Run* (New Jersey: Bridge Publishing, Inc., 1968), 107.

Chapter 8

THE LEADING
OF THE SPIRIT

"We interrupt this program to bring you an important announcement...." It can be annoying to hear that announced in the middle of your favorite television show. Breaking news alerts notify us of approaching storms or high winds. If there is a potential tornado or hurricane headed your way, you may not mind having your favorite show interrupted so that your life can be saved. However, if you're the type who plans out your life down to the last minute, any change in that plan could be frustrating. But being led by the Spirit may mean changing your course with little advance notice. Take for instance the following remarkable story of our friend Donna, a wife and mother, whose sensitivity to the voice of God guided her family to safety.

With her husband, Neal, working for a government department in Afghanistan, Donna learned to daily confess for herself and her family that they were "in the right place at the right time" and that their "footsteps are ordered by God" (Ps. 37:23). In July 2005, after a family vacation in Dubai (United Arab Emirates), where they met up with Neal, Donna and her three grown children decided to end their trip by stopping off in

London before going home. They arrived on July 6 and spent time in London shopping and taking in the sites.

The following day, on July 7, they were scheduled to fly out at around 3:00 in the afternoon, but at breakfast in the hotel, around 7:30 A.M., she heard inside of her spirit: "You need to leave now." The airport was only an hour away from the hotel, but she knew that she heard that they were to leave right then. She told her kids to get their luggage after breakfast, and to her amazement they didn't even ask why. They went up to their room, packed their bags, and headed to the "tube" (subway).

It was morning rush hour. The subway should have been coming at regular intervals, but none came. They heard over the intercom that this particular line was not running and that they needed to get on a different subway. What they didn't know at the time was that this subway had just been bombed by terrorists. When they got to the other station, a subway came but it was overcrowded. Her oldest daughter was able to get on, but there wasn't room for the rest of the family. When she realized that they could be separated from each other, Donna yelled to her daughter to get off the subway. Thankfully, she made her way off the subway before it left the station. They were able to get on the new subway and took it to the next stop where it came to a halt. They sat there for ten minutes.

About that time, they were told to get off the subway car and that they needed to evacuate the subway station due to a security incident. No one knew what was going on. They got out onto the street and saw police officers and ambulances going every direction. Something was up, but they didn't know what. They were in the middle of all these commuters who were on their way to work. People were on their cell phones and rumors were flying about what was happening, but no one really knew at that point. Donna and her kids were advised to get on a city bus to get to Victoria train station, which would eventually get them to the airport. They got on the bus and transferred to another bus. They arrived at the train station just as they announced there would be no more bus service because a bomb had exploded on a city bus. When they arrived at the overcrowded train station, they were still thirty miles from the airport. The public transportation in London was slowing down, causing a bottleneck. Thankfully, they were able to catch a train to Gatwick Airport. Just as they arrived at the airport, it was announced that the trains were being shut down. Once again, they had been just one step ahead of where they needed to be.

Psalm 37:23 says, "The steps of a good man are ordered by the Lord," but it wasn't until they landed in the U.S. that they understood how well the Lord had directed them. As they pulled out their subway tickets from that morning, they realized that one of the many bombs that went off in London was at 8:50 A.M. at the subway station that they had passed through just ten minutes before it exploded. They had missed that bombing by ten minutes. If they had not left at the inconvenient time that the Lord told them to leave that morning, they could have possibly been in the middle of that situation.

We all want to hear from the Spirit of God as accurately as Donna did if we are ever in a terror situation. God is sending signals and directions to us on a regular basis. Do you hear them? When you tune into the "station" where He's broadcasting, your "receiver" will pick up the signal, and instead of "static" on your end, you'll hear clearly what the Spirit of God is saying.

STAY TUNED

Noah built an ark the size of a football field strictly on a word from the Lord. No one, including him, had ever seen rain before, much less a flood. His neighbors made fun of him and laughed at his construction project. But Noah lived by faith. He heard the audible voice of God, and he obeyed, and as a result, he and his family were the only people who escaped when the earth was flooded (see Gen. 6-8). Hearing from the Spirit of God is vital in the days in which we live. It can literally mean the difference between life and death. The method that God used to save Noah was an audible voice; for Donna, it was by words that welled up within her by the Holy Spirit. There is no set way for every circumstance, and He may lead in different ways on various occasions. He is Supreme and can use whichever method He chooses; our job is to hear Him accurately. It takes humility to bypass our senses and listen to further instruction from the Spirit of God. Sometimes the Spirit of God can lead us completely opposite of how we "feel" we should go. It's at those times that the Lord will confirm our steps as we begin to follow His direction.

Because you have a relationship with God, He's going to talk to you. The Lord may tell you, "Take this direction...go this way...don't go there...go here." When you're leading your small children, sometimes you speak to them gently by saying, "Come here." Sometimes you may reach to hold their hand in a busy traffic area. And sometimes you may have to shout to get their attention if they're headed for danger. The main thing is this: You'll find a way to get their attention because they're your children, and you love them, and don't want to see them hurt. The Holy Spirit is no different. He will find a way to reach you and get you the information you need at the time you need it. He is not hiding Himself from you. Go where God leads you because the safest place on earth for you is in the center of the will of God.

THE WORD OF GOD

The most reliable way to be led by the Spirit is through the written Word of God. There will be times when we won't always see with our natural eye what is going to take place. This is when Christians must live by faith in the promises of God, which are in His Word. In Matthew 4:4, Jesus said, "Man shall not live by bread alone, but by every word that proceeds from the mouth of God." The written Word came about when holy men of God wrote as they were led by the Spirit of God (see 2 Pet. 1:21). If you find yourself always questioning the Word of God and its authority, you will have no authority to resist fear. The world system is constantly coming against the Word and creating confusion in believers and non-believers alike. As a result, people lack peace and faith at times when they need it. Make a decision to believe that God's Word is the absolute truth. Don't question its validity. It is the only stable factor that you have while living here on earth. Mark 13:31 says, "Heaven and earth will pass away, but My words will by no means pass away."

Like a precision tool of a master craftsman, the Word of God can slice through our ideas and motives to reveal the hidden plan of God. The book of Hebrews says that it is "...living and powerful, and sharper than any two-edged sword, piercing even to the division of soul and spirit, and of joints and marrow, and is a discerner of the thoughts and intents of the heart"

(Heb. 4:12). As you read God's Word, God's Word will read you—your motives and your thoughts—and will help you to discern your circumstances. God's Word will guide you. It is an accurate guide to settle the issues in our hearts. His Word is a lamp to your feet and a light to your path (see Ps. 119:105).

After holding our first crusade in Russia, in 1991, I had great compassion for the people. They were so hungry for God. I asked the Lord on the plane ride home if and when we should return. I didn't know what to do, but as I read the Bible that day, Acts 18:11 seemed to leap off the page at me: "And he continued there a year and six months, teaching the word of God among them." Immediately I knew in my spirit that the Lord was leading us to be in St. Petersburg, Russia, for one week in eighteen consecutive months. I had complete peace that the Lord had led me to that answer. We followed through with that direction from the Lord and had complete peace about it. At the same time, the government of the Soviet Union was on very shaky ground. If we had looked with our eyes, we might have changed our decision. But because we followed His leading through the Word of God and the peace that followed, we saw thousands of Russians give their hearts to the Lord.

Many people are led by fear. They're afraid to go anywhere. They won't do anything. They won't step out because fear has put them in a box. By reading and hearing the Word of God on a regular basis, we can build up a "reserve" inside of us that can lead us on short notice when necessary. It becomes instant recall as the Lord brings a Scripture to our hearts at the most opportune time to lead us into His plan.

PEACE OR LACK OF IT

Having a sense of peace about a situation can also be a leading of the Spirit. Philippians says that we should not to be anxious but that we should pray about every situation. When we do this, "the peace of God, which surpasses all understanding, will guard your hearts and minds through Christ Jesus" (Phil. 4:7). His peace will be evident to everyone around you.

The Lord can also lead us by the lack of peace in certain situations. We've had that happen with us at times when we knew that we were not supposed to do what others wanted us to do or to go certain places where we had been invited. We had prayed about it, and we had uneasiness in our hearts. The peace was missing. We may not always know why the Lord leads us to not go somewhere or with certain people, but it's wise to heed His direction, even if it means going against what someone feels you should do. It's worth it every time. God can deal with the other person and work it out in them as well.

WORDS SPOKEN BY THE HOLY SPIRIT

Just as Donna in the earlier part of this chapter heard specific words from the Holy Spirit, which guided her to safety in her travel, we know of a young man who was about to board a plane in Miami when he distinctly heard in his heart, "Don't get on that plane." He and his friend were scheduled for that flight, and they had their tickets checked and their baggage on the plane already. But they felt like the Lord told them to go to the Ft. Lauderdale airport to fly out instead, which was about 30 minutes away from where they were. They followed the words from the Holy Spirit, retrieved their luggage, and went over to the other airport to fly back to their destination. Another couple who was waiting to get on the plane was so glad that two seats had suddenly become available, so they rushed to check in their baggage and were the last passengers on the flight. That was May 11, 1996, the day that ValuJet flight 592—the flight they were scheduled to be on—headed out of Miami and crashed in the Florida Everglades. There were no survivors.

When the crash happened, the parents of this young man knew that he was supposed to be on that flight. They didn't hear from him, but they saw the news. They just began praying in the Spirit, clutching each other's hands for hours. They had stood on the Word of Psalm 91 that no evil would befall their family and that they would be delivered. Hours went by without any word from their son, but they continued to stand on the Word of God. The young man didn't know what had happened because he had gone on the flight out of Ft. Lauderdale instead of Miami. He didn't see the news until he landed. When he finally landed, he called his parents to tell them he was safe. His parents were ecstatic to hear his voice and to learn of how he had followed the leading of the Holy Spirit's words in his heart.

VISIONS AND DREAMS

You can't do anything that will make the Holy Spirit speak one way or the other, so don't reject the different ways that the Holy Spirit leads. God is very creative. We would be foolish to demand that He speak to us in a certain way. The key is to just be open to whichever way He chooses and obey it.

When I met Sharon, she was sixteen and I was seventeen years old. A year later, I was saved and became fired up in my walk with the Lord. As I went on a family road trip to Florida, I looked out the window as we were driving and saw a vision of Sharon and me on a large stage ministering to people. It was the first time that I had ever seen an open vision, like a video screen, in front of my eyes. I had to blink to find out if what I was seeing was just in my head. I had no teaching or experience in visions. I wasn't even thinking about her other than as a friend. That vision sparked something in me, however, and I invited her for a date when I got back in town. I didn't tell her the vision until after we had been dating for about two years. The vision was tested before we married, which helped us to know even more that God had called us together. That vision helped to lead each of us to the right mate.

God has a plan to accomplish His will in the earth, and you are part of that plan. He may be instructing you to go somewhere that you have never thought about going. Your obedience to His guidance can change your destiny and affect a nation. Don't insist on having a vision where you "see" things. Just say, "Father, I am ready and willing to hear Your voice," and He will honor your desire in His perfect way. Not everyone will have visions, but all of us can be led by God's Spirit.

The book of Acts records a vision that Peter had that ultimately directed his entire ministry after that point. He believed that salvation was only for the Jewish people. In the vision, he saw Heaven opened, and a sheet filled with "unclean" animals was let down. He heard a voice tell him to eat, but Peter defiantly said "No!" The Lord responded by telling him that "what God has cleansed you must not call common" (Acts 10:15). This took place three times in the vision, and then he awoke. Through an angelic visitation, days earlier, Cornelius in Caesarea was told to send for Peter in Joppa and invite him to his home. The angel told Cornelius where Peter was staying, although they did not even know each other at the time. God was working out a plan for the Gentiles to hear the gospel, but it was dependent upon Peter following the leading of the Spirit of God. Peter's act of obedience to go to Caesarea with people he did not even know opened the doors for the Gospel to be preached to the Gentiles. I am very thankful that Peter obeyed!

PRACTICE INSTANT OBEDIENCE

Instantly obeying the voice of the Holy Spirit is crucial. It could be the difference between living here on this earth and meeting God face to face a little sooner than expected. It could also mean fulfilling your destiny or living a life of despair because of not obeying what you knew God said to do. As you read His Word, begin to do what the Word says. That will train your human spirit to obey the Spirit of God. The more it is trained, the easier it will be to obey in other ways that the Spirit prompts you.

When our children were little, we worked at training them to obey us the first time we asked. We didn't raise our voice at them and scream for them or count to ten. We did have to discipline them for disobedience in order to teach them boundaries. After each time of discipline, we hugged them and told them we loved them. It was important for us to teach them to instantly obey because we felt that it prepared them to learn how to obey God later on in life. As parents, we can tell you that it has definitely paid off for our children. One such incident involves our oldest daughter's protection when we were not around to guide her.

Sarah was about three years old and had somehow slipped past Sharon one day, and she got out the front door. She had seen a little kitty cat across the street, and she started running down our front yard toward the kitten. Sharon looked out the window just in time to see her stop suddenly at the edge of the curb. Before she could even get out the door, a car came speeding down the street and zoomed right past Sarah. Sharon didn't know, until she ran outside to get Sarah, that our neighbor across the street had just walked out on her front porch when she saw Sarah running down the yard and the car simultaneously speeding down the street. She had yelled, "Sarah! Stop!" At that moment, Sarah stopped, and the car went right past her. We were so thankful for those neighbors! Sarah's obedience saved her life that day.

YOU CAN BE LED BY THE SPIRIT

As you learn to heed His voice, you will know His direction and guidance in the location that you're to be in and the people that you're to be with. Raise your faith level in the ability that God has to speak to you and in the ability that you have to hear Him. God has all the ability, but you have to have faith in your ability to hear God's voice.

In any of these leadings of the Holy Spirit, God will always provide a plan of action or a way of escape to those who will listen to His voice and obey Him. I don't advocate that people just randomly go out and do anything they want to do, violating natural laws, the Holy Spirit's leading, or the Word of God.

You have to listen to the Holy Spirit, put God's Word in your heart, and walk by it. You may have to go into an environment where some terrible events have taken place, but you don't have to have a spirit of fear. If you must go into those areas for some reason, listen to the Holy Spirit and what He leads you to do. If you're going into an area that's not considered dangerous, but you sense you shouldn't be going, then don't. We've counseled and prayed with individuals who have rejected those inner promptings of the Holy Spirit and have found themselves in disastrous situations.

I remember hearing the story, years ago, of a single parent mom who had promised to help her friend who was leaving town for a few days by picking up her mail and watering her plants in her home. The woman's husband had not gone on the trip with his wife and had stayed home to work while she was gone. When our friend went to check on the house, she found that her friend's husband was home and had a beer in his hand when he came to the door. Our friend offered to come back at another time, and he said, "No, it's okay. Come on in and water the plants." Because she had her son with her, she reasoned that it would be okay to enter the house. She wasn't afraid because she remembered the Scripture of Second Timothy 1:7 that God had not given her a spirit of fear, but power, love, and a sound mind. Once she got inside the house, her son went to a toy box to play, but the man shoved her into a room and violated her.

Later she came to talk with Sharon and asked, "How did that happen? I pray Scripture daily and read my Bible daily." When Sharon asked her to retell the story, she realized that when she first approached the door and the man answered, she had an uneasy feeling inside. She felt that she should leave and come back later, but the man reasoned with her to stay. That uneasy feeling was the leading of the Holy Spirit prompting her to get away. Even though she was reminded of the Scripture from Second Timothy 1:7 when she went into the house, we must remember that the devil quoted a Scripture to Jesus in Matthew 4, while He was in the wilderness, to try to convince Him to do what he wanted Him to do (see Matt. 4:1-11).

The Holy Spirit is inside of us as believers, prompting us to avoid danger and to go another direction. We need to listen to that inner voice in our thoughts and discern the circumstances in which we find ourselves. Let the Holy Spirit be your navigator. He knows where you should be and when you should be there, and He won't lead you down the wrong path.

Chapter 9

WARNINGS FROM GOD

Traveling to other countries to present the gospel has been a regular part of our ministry since we first began in 1976. We wanted our children to experience the joy of sharing the good news on foreign soil as well so we began bringing them with us when they were very young. As a result, each of our four children has had a passion for missions birthed in them.

Our oldest daughter, Sarah, is now married, and she and her husband head up our teen mission groups that go out on spring break and summer trips to other nations every year. Our Christian school takes the sixth graders on their first mission trip into Mexico. It's a great experience for the children as they take the gospel for the first time into a country where people speak a different language. Our teens must rely on the Lord to help them. For many of the teens it's their first time away from home without their parents. Speaking of the parents, we understand what they go through as they release their precious sons and daughters to minister in another country.

When Sarah was going on her sixth-grade mission trip—the first one without her family accompanying her—Sharon really had to fight against the fear of something happening to her on the trip. Someone had shared with her a story that had been on the news months before about a group that had gone into Mexico and one of the team had been kidnapped. A few days before the class was scheduled to head out to Mexico, Sharon had a dream in which Sarah was kidnapped on the mission trip. When she awoke and told me, she wanted me to call off the trip for the class right away.

It is in these sorts of situations that you must discern your thoughts and dreams. What have you been listening to? Have you been meditating on negative news? We must guard our hearts by protecting what goes into our eye gates and ear gates. I had to discern Sharon's dream, whether it was from God or whether it was a negative thought of the enemy. I did not have any kind of urging in my spirit to call off the trip at this point. I respect Sharon and know that she hears from the Lord, but I also knew that she was dealing with a lot of fear about Sarah going on this trip without us. I told Sharon, "Honey, until God speaks to me, I'm not going to stop this trip. If God speaks to you and me between now and the time they leave, I'll put a stop to it." I didn't hear any change of direction from God or Sharon. She didn't have any more dreams. I didn't feel that we were to put a stop to it, so we let Sarah go with the team. Consequently, no dangerous situations presented themselves on the trip. Praise God!

What Sharon had been dealing with was fear-based thoughts or what the Bible calls "lying imaginations." Those thoughts became so strong in her that they even affected her dreams at night. She realized that what she had been doing was rehearsing a lie in her head that tried to stop a group from spreading the gospel. We have to bring our thoughts captive to the Lord and meditate on what God has promised and then listen to the still, small voice of the Holy Spirit within our hearts.

TWO KINDS OF STRONGHOLDS

A stronghold is formed in a person's mind when they continually meditate on a particular thought. You can have a stronghold of faith or a stronghold of fear depending on what you're thinking about. Thoughts that are contrary to the Word of God form strongholds of fear. The good news is that God has given us a method to take control of those thoughts. Second Corinthians 10:4-5 says, "For the weapons of our warfare are not carnal but mighty in God for pulling down strongholds, casting down arguments and every high thing that exalts itself against the knowledge of God, bringing every thought into captivity to the obedience of Christ." We take control over our thoughts and make them agree with the Word of God instead of our feelings and emotions.

On the other hand, a stronghold of faith (or truth) can be formed by believing, speaking, and acting on the Word of God. It will overcome doubts and concerns and set up strength inside of your spirit. When considering the protection of the Lord over us in this world, Psalm 121:8 declares, "The Lord shall preserve your going out and your coming in from this time forth, and even forevermore." The word *preserve* means "to keep you from all harm." To guard, protect, and deliver is God's will for you. You might not know if you're coming or going, but either way, God will protect you. Develop a faith stronghold based upon the promises of God's Word.

GOD'S WARNING SYSTEMS

So how can you know the difference between fear-based thoughts and true warnings from the Lord? It begins by learning to hear from the Spirit of God on a regular basis. By the mercy and love of God, He is sending warnings to each of us. You have to interpret and respond appropriately—not in fear or terror—but in faith. There are natural warnings that God many times will use to get our attention. They may come in the form of a siren or some type of alarm. Living in the Midwest in the United States, we're familiar with tornado sirens, and we appreciate the advance notice that tells us to take cover. It's important to be alert when God is trying to send a signal your way. It could be the difference between life and death. Our family almost missed a warning altogether. It could have been devastating for us.

Back in 1991, I had purchased a couple of smoke alarms for our house. I came home with the package and was too busy to install them at the time, so I put them on the top shelf in the laundry room. A few months passed, and I noticed them sitting on that shelf. Once again, I didn't have enough time to install them on the ceiling, but I thought I better at least get the batteries in them. I took them out of their boxes, put the batteries in them, and put them back on the shelf. A few days later, on a cool October night, around 2 A.M., those smoke detectors paid off. I was suddenly awakened by a loud, monotonous noise. At first I thought it was our daughter Ruthie's alarm clock. I didn't know what time it was because it was still dark outside, but I figured it would wake her up shortly and she'd turn it off. The annoying sound didn't stop. *When is she going to turn that thing off?* I just wanted to get back to sleep.

Realizing that no one was budging to turn off the alarm, I started to get up to take care of it myself. As I sat up in bed, I looked around and saw that everything in the room was hazy.

I breathed in and started choking on the heavy smoke in the room. That irritating sound was the smoke alarms on that top shelf of the laundry room! Our house was on fire! I jumped up and started screaming, "Get out! There's a fire! Get out!" Miraculously, we got out through the front door and stood on the driveway, praising God that we were delivered from the fire! What a relief! It was dark, and we were all screaming, but in the chaos, Sharon and I, along with Sarah who was about twelve at the time, and our seven-year-old son John, started looking around to make sure that everyone was there.

Sharon screamed, "Ruthie! Where's Ruthie? She's still inside!" We couldn't find our ten-year-old daughter. I ran back to the house and went through the front door as flames blazed through the roof. I couldn't see anything in the house because of the dense smoke, and I started feeling for her. I touched her head and felt relief as I dragged her out by her long hair. She was a little shaken up from the rescue, but she was safe. I had time to rest just a few seconds when we realized our six-year-old Paul was nowhere to be found. We started screaming for him, but he didn't answer. Sharon yelled, "Paul is still inside!" My lungs were burning from the hot smoke, but without hesitation, I ran up to the door again and forced it open. The house was engulfed in flames, but I had to get my son! As I groped the walls of the house down the hall, I reached down and felt the top of Paul's head. He had learned to "stop, drop, and roll," so he was obediently crawling on the floor. I grabbed him and scooped him out of the house.

We walked across the street to our neighbors, the Browns. As we sat on their front porch, watching the house burn, the fire trucks and emergency vehicles began arriving. They expected that whoever had been in that house would not be coming out alive. But God had delivered us! We lost our personal belongings that night, but our lives were miraculously spared. A believer may experience setbacks and afflictions, "but the Lord delivers him out of them all" (Ps. 34:19). It's important for us not to ignore the signals that are intended to help us avert danger. That man-made device was used to save our lives that night, but it was the Spirit of God who told me to buy it and to put batteries in it. Although I did not install them in the ceiling as I should have, I am grateful to God for His mercy.

HOW WILL I KNOW IF GOD IS WARNING *ME*?

Some people may wonder if they would know the difference between a warning from God and just fearful thoughts. Our friend Patty is a Christian, and she wondered the very same thing. She was fearful of flying in airplanes because her first plane ride was very turbulent. Flying in an airplane became a struggle for her after that incident. As a Christian, it bothered her that she was so fearful of flying. She had a close relationship with the Lord, but that didn't combat the terror that she experienced every time she boarded a plane. Patty's story follows:

> Every time I would fly, I felt anxious and would pray continually. I'd look around at other people on the plane and couldn't believe they weren't praying. People would be calmly reading their magazines or books, and I would think, "What are you doing! Why aren't you

praying?" It was such a big deal to me that I couldn't imagine others didn't feel the same.

I didn't want to be afraid, but I was. I would always hear ministers say that God would speak to us to warn us if we're not supposed to fly on an airplane or take a particular flight. I knew how to hear His voice in other areas of my life, but I was really concerned that my fear of flying would get in the way of my hearing directly from Heaven. I was anxious about flying on *any* plane, so how would I know whether it was my fear talking or God warning me?

Several years ago, as we were getting ready to fly to see my mom in Ohio, I felt like I had to settle this with the Lord. I prayed, "Lord, how am I ever going to know the difference between my own anxiousness and when you're speaking, saying, 'Warning! Warning! Get off the plane'? I *really* want to know the difference." So God created a situation for me to learn the difference.

We flew to my mom's, and everything was fine, although I was anxious the whole time, and I was very thankful to get off the plane. But on our return flight, our plane landed in St. Louis for a short layover. We were supposed to stay on this plane, and as I was sitting there, my heart was beating so fast. Somehow I just knew something was wrong with the plane. I was praying in the spirit, and I looked around the plane. Everyone was peaceful and, as usual, just reading their books and magazines. I said to the Lord, "Is this You talking to me? What is going on?" All of a sudden I had this knowing that something was wrong. It was different from my anxious feeling I would get.

We weren't supposed to be getting off the plane during this layover, but somebody got sick and they wanted to get that person out, so they let all of us off the plane. I was standing by the window looking out at the plane, and I had no peace. I kept thinking that something was wrong.

As I got back on the plane, I continued praying. I leaned over to my son and said, "Michael, pray. Something's wrong. I just feel like something's wrong." I began praying, "God, don't let this plane take off if there's something wrong. There are all these people, and they don't know You. Please don't let us take off."

The plane got ready to take off, and I was still feeling like something was wrong. We backed up, and we got half-way out to the runway, and all of a sudden they turned back. Over the intercom, the pilot announced, "We're sorry, but there's something wrong with the plane. We're going to have to delay takeoff." Whew! I said to the Lord, "Oh, thank You, Jesus." But I still didn't lose the knowing that there was something wrong.

As we were sitting there while they checked out the plane, I said, "Okay, God, this plane is going to crash, isn't it? Do You want me to stand up and preach now? Or do I wait until we're on our way down and stand up and say, 'Okay, everybody, now is a good time to know Jesus'?" I just felt like I had to let this whole plane full of people know about Jesus and so I was preparing myself with Scriptures and a whole plan to preach to them. I just knew we were all going to die, but I wasn't afraid of dying.

However, I was still praying that God would change something. They had apparently checked out what they thought was wrong with the plane, and they closed the door and got ready for takeoff.

Suddenly this lady in front of me ran up to the flight attendant and said, "Let me off of this plane." The flight attendant said, "I can't do that because the door is shut and we're getting ready to fly out." The passenger said, "No, you don't understand. I had a dream, and in this dream the engine fell off and the plane crashed. I'm not saying it's this plane, but I don't have peace, so I'm getting off of this plane."

The flight attendant had to tell the pilot why the lady was so anxious and wanted off the plane. She told him that the passenger had had a dream about an engine falling off a plane. They had checked other things out on the plane, but because of the lady's anxiousness and the dream she said she had, the pilot decided to hold off and have the engines checked. When they did that one last check, the mechanics found a crack in the engine.

If we had gone up in that airplane, the engine would have fallen off. The flight attendant later came to the woman in front of me and thanked her. She told her that we would surely have all died and that the woman had saved all of our lives.

They put us on another plane, and I lost that feeling that something was wrong. It was just gone. I had total peace. We got back to Tulsa, and I thought, "Oh, that's what it feels like. That's what it's like when the Lord is talking to me and warning when something is wrong on a plane."

Ever since, I have never had fear or anxiousness about flying. I actually love flying now. Now I know what God's voice feels like inside of me because what He was telling me was true.

Just like God made a way of escape for Patty, He'll do the same for you if you are ever in a dangerous situation. The more you take the time to learn His Word, the more you'll be able to know His voice when He speaks within your spirit. If you're unsure about whether you're just feeling afraid or if something is wrong in your situation, ask the Lord to help you. He won't hide His will and direction from you. He wants to guide you into safety and preserve your life. He has a myriad of ways to get the message to you; so you can know that your steps are truly ordered of Him. It is important to know the difference between the spirit of fear and a warning from God.

Chapter 10

PUT THE ANGELS TO WORK

All I knew about angels when I was growing up was what I saw on Valentine's Day cards. They were always pictured as happy, fat babies with bows and arrows. I was told that they went around shooting people with arrows, causing love to somehow well up inside of those who had been hit. I had never seen that happen.

When you read the Bible, you will realize that there are no angels that are in baby form. The angels of the Bible are all in adult form, and it seems that they appeared to people in a masculine form with great strength that was awesome and even fearful to people. Their first words to the humans were always, "Fear not." They came to assure humans that they did not have to fear because God was with them.

Many of us know that there have been times when we have been delivered from unexplainable near-misses and possible accidents. Circumstances surrounding the way we came out without a scratch have attested to the reality that God had intervened in some way for our protection. There is no other explanation except that God worked supernaturally to deliver our lives.

The world has its own ideas of who angels are and what they do. *Touched by an Angel* became a hit television show several years ago as week after week "angels" discreetly appeared in people's lives to help them through major crises. And there was Clarence in the 1946 classic *It's a Wonderful Life*. It could be that these interpretations of angelic visitations came from Hebrews 13:2, where we're told to be kind to strangers because some people have found that strangers were actually angels sent by God. Obviously, the world's ideas and portrayal of angels are generally a reflection of man's view. However, people want to know that God will intervene in their lives and save them in impossible circumstances. These stories and others like them portrayed God's love to man through His messengers. Minds and hearts are touched to believe that God loves them enough to send help at critical moments in their lives, although what you've seen about angels on the television screen is not entirely accurate.

God has put together a fantastic plan of delivering people from calamities. Not only has He given us the Holy Spirit to lead us, but He has angels on assignment to deliver and uphold us. He created them to work for you. This is Bible truth in which you can trust.

ANGELS ON ASSIGNMENT

In Hebrews, it says of angels, "Are they not all ministering spirits sent forth to minister for those who will inherit salvation" (Heb. 1:14). Ministering spirits are "serving" spirits for divine purposes. The angels aid those who are heirs of salvation in the earth. When you believe God, though you don't see them, angelic hosts are released who move at the speed of light to operate in your behalf. Whether you see them or feel them makes no difference.

Just like a military has troops in place for various aspects of combat, angels have special assignments and responsibilities. Warring angels battle in the heavenlies. A reference is made in Jude 9 to Michael, the archangel, contending with the devil. When Daniel received visions regarding the end times, an angel identified as Gabriel was dispatched to bring him understanding of the visions (see Dan. 9:21). This angel was delayed because of a battle with the demonic prince of Persia who would not let him through. Michael the archangel had to step in and help fight with Gabriel so that he could get through with his message to Daniel (see Dan. 10).

Messenger angels are found throughout the Bible. Mary received instruction from the angel Gabriel when she was told that she would be the mother of Jesus (see Luke 1:26-30). It is also recorded that Joseph received direction from angels on three different occasions: when he was told to take Mary as his wife (see Matt. 1:24), when he was warned to leave Bethlehem for Egypt because of King Herod's order to kill the male babies (see Matt. 2:13), and when they were to return to Israel and settle in Nazareth (see Matt. 2:19).

In May of 1993, while we were holding a week of meetings preaching in St. Petersburg, Russia, I preached on the Second Coming of Jesus Christ and the events that would precede Jesus' return. A family who attended the meeting that evening went home after the service, and when they opened the door to their apartment, two men in glistening white apparel stood before them. They said, "The man you heard preach tonight is my messenger, and you can believe his words. Jesus Christ is returning soon." The father, mother, and their two children said that as soon as these men finished speaking, they disappeared before their eyes. God sent these angels to confirm the gospel that we had preached.

Angels are also deliverers sent to protect and guard us, which is the focus of this chapter. Daniel was delivered from hungry lions by an angel who shut their mouths through the night (see Dan. 6:22). When Peter was put in jail and was being guarded by sixteen soldiers, he was supernaturally delivered by an angel (see Acts 12). The ministry of angels to guard and save us in times of distress didn't end with the book of Acts. It's still happening today. Such is the case for a woman we know named Doris, who experienced an angel's help when she dived into shallow water at a nearby lake. She hit her head on a submerged rock and immediately became paralyzed. With her face down in the water, she was unable to move or breathe. She desperately prayed to God to save her, and within moments someone turned her over so she could breathe. He began to give instruction to those around. He was there when the ambulance came. She never saw the person come or go, but eventually other people began to gather around her to help. When she asked them about the person who had turned her over in the water, no one knew who she was talking about. It was as if he had disappeared into thin air. She tried to find out later who he was, but was unsuccessful. Doris was treated for her injuries and over a period of time became a walking miracle, thanks to an angel that intervened on her behalf.

Angels are guarding us even when we're unaware of their presence. I'll never forget one particular story of angelic protection that we heard from some missionaries in Mexico. There was a village in Mexico that had been reached with the gospel, and a group of the villagers had come to Christ. The village had a mixture of all types of false religion and witch-craft, so the Christians began to live together in little huts on the hillside, away from the village. There was great animosity from the religious leader in the village toward those that had been born again. (They called the Christians the "born-agains.") One night, the religious leader got some of the villagers drunk, gave them all machetes, and stirred them up to kill everyone on the side of the hill in those huts. Well, nothing happened that night.

The next day all of these Christians came down to the village square to do their shopping, and people began to ask them, "Where did those men in white suits come from?" They said, "What?" And they said, "In the middle of the night, as these folks were walking up the hill with their machetes, suddenly the whole hillside lit up and in front of every hut was a huge white being with a drawn sword." Thank God for angels!

We are grateful for the ministry of angels; however, we are warned not to worship them. When the angel came to the apostle John with visions of the end times, he fell down to worship the angel. The angel forbid him, saying, "See that you do not do that. For I am your fellow servant, and of your brethren the prophets, and of those who keep the words of this book. Worship God" (Rev. 22:9).

PUTTING THE ANGELS TO WORK FOR YOU

Angels have been given parameters in responding to our needs. Psalm 103:20 says that angels move in response to hearing the Word of God: "Bless the Lord, you His angels, who excel in strength, who do His word, heeding the voice of His word." When you are speaking God's Word, you become the voice of His Word. The angels carry out or perform the Word that's spoken. That's why we don't just read the promises of God; we *say* them: "Lord, You are my refuge." Suddenly we have the angels' attention because they hearken to the voice of God's Word. When you keep your mouth shut and you don't speak the Word of God, it's like the angels just have to fold their wings and watch.

You can release the angels to minister on your behalf and for others as well. I remember one incident several years ago when I was driving down the highway and a car passed me (going in the same direction) at about 90 miles an hour. The moment he passed me, I knew that he was headed for a crash if he wasn't stopped. And I just loosed my angels and said, "Angels, go get him!" Not far from where I was, there's a part of that stretch of highway that curves onto an overpass. When he came to that curve, he missed the turn. He went off the side of the road and the car rolled all the way down the hill and landed in a grassy area on its wheels. I saw the accident happen because I was behind him. I parked, jumped out, and ran down the hill to check on the guy. Dazed, the man was sitting in the backseat of the car, not really knowing what had happened to him or how he got there. The car was upright, and as he was looking out the backseat window at me. I said, "God saved your life!" Still in a state of shock, he said, "I know it."

When a tragedy strikes, sometimes people question, "Where were the angels? I thought the angels were surrounding people." But according to Psalm 103, the angels hearken to the voice of God's Word. Other times people say, "Well, there are just so many things we don't understand that happen in life." That's true. There are some things we don't understand. But we ought to work with the things that we do understand. And since the angels hearken to the voice of God's Word, we ought to learn how to speak it so that we can have their help when we need it. We can call upon the help of angels by declaring God's Word daily: "Lord, thank You that You give Your angels charge over me and my family, keeping us in all of our ways." (See Psalm 91:11.)

Chapter 11

SPEAKING THE PROMISES OF PROTECTION

The power of words is immeasurable. If you think they don't matter, think again. Positive or negative, we are living in the sum total of the words that we have spoken up to this point. "Death and life are in the power of the tongue," says Proverbs 18:21. What you say is very important. In fact, we will give account on the Day of Judgment for every idle word that we have spoken—any useless, unproductive word (see Matt. 12:36). The angels take notice of what we say, and so does the devil.

Staying free of the fear of terror has much to do with what you're saying about yourself and your situation. Continually telling people how afraid you are will negate the power of the love of God to free you from fear. You'll see yourself as inferior and weak, as someone who is cowering and losing in life. However, victory is won as you speak Scriptures (words of life) over your situation. The Word of God is that life-giver and is anointed and powerful when you read it and speak it. When you speak it, God's Word goes from just being a history lesson to becoming a living Word that you live by. It will cause you to see yourself rising up to the level of an overcomer—perfectly positioned to carry out God's plan for your life. To combat thoughts of fear and terror that may still linger, Psalm 91 will keep you grounded in His protection over you.

Moses wrote Psalm 91 as the children of Israel departed from the land of Egypt and were about to begin their trek across the desert. It was God's revelation of what He had done for them in their deliverance from Egypt, but it was also a promise of what He would do for them in their future. They could stand upon this word in the most difficult circumstances, and God would deliver them. That same psalm is a picture of God's protection over His people today.

During the Gulf War, in the early 1990s, we heard about a group of young men who became known as the "Psalm 91 Battalion." They quoted this psalm together every day. They carried it on a little card in their pockets, along with a small New Testament that included the Psalms. That battalion did not have one fatality during the war.

Verse 1 of Psalm 91 begins "He who dwells in the secret place of the Most High shall abide under the shadow of the Almighty." The Hebrew word for "dwell" is *yashab*, which means "to sit down; to remain; to settle in the sense of taking up a homestead or staking out a claim and resisting all claim-jumpers; to possess a place and live therein"[1] This indicates that we must have an aggressive attitude about keeping our lives submitted to God and not allowing the devil to intimidate us or attack us. Abiding under the shadow of the Almighty is a picture of a father protecting a son or an eagle protecting its little eaglets. When you're under that shadow, you're very close. When you are in that overshadowing presence, you are defended.

But where is this secret place so that we can go there and be protected? We may think of Heaven as the secret place of the Most High, the very throne of God. On earth, when the Israelites built a tabernacle, they were instructed to put a place in it called the Most Holy Place or the Holy of Holies. Later, in a temple in Jerusalem, when Jesus died on the cross and gave His blood for our sins, the veil of that temple was torn in two from top to bottom. It symbolized that the Holy of Holies was no longer in a tent or a building; it was to be in people. (See 1 Kings 6:16; Matthew 27:50-51.) You are that temple of the Holy Ghost.

Just being a church member of a Bible-believing congregation does not mean that you're dwelling in the secret place of the Most High. It does not just happen because you have a Bible or because your mother and father were Christians. Dwelling in the secret place happens when you make a decision to put your life in His hands and you allow His Spirit to rule in your life. In that intimate place, you have communion with the Lord on a daily basis. I'm not talking about the "act of communion" when you go to a church service and take a cup and a wafer that represent the blood and body of the Lord Jesus. That is important and not to be taken lightly. However, the communion that I'm referring to is the interchange of God speaking, you hearing Him, and you doing what He says, as well as you speaking to God and knowing that He hears you. That exchange goes back and forth in a person who is "dwelling in the secret place." When your heart is sensitive to His promptings in order to obey His leading, you'll stay protected.

When you dwell somewhere, that means you stay put. It's not an in-and-out situation or an occasional visit like you might drop into a hotel every now and then. It's not a weekend stay or a Sunday morning relationship. Dwelling somewhere means a constant, ongoing, ever-present relationship. It's when we *surrender* our lives before the Lord, saying, "Not my will but Thy will" (see Luke 22:42). A person can know about God, can actually believe that God is, and yet not be surrendered. People who are surrendered are usable by the Lord. They're ready to serve the Lord and to do whatever He says. When He's Lord, that means that He's exalted. It means that you have humbled yourself, that you have come down and that He's come up. It means that you've submitted your life. It's not a rebellious attitude of doing things your own way. No, it's totally laying down your life for Him. When you have surrendered to the Lord in this way, you have *complete trust* in Him. He's going to show you where to be and when to be there. You can trust Him.

It is the place where you have *received His love* into your heart. You have accepted Him and chosen to respond with your total love to Him. When you realize that God loves you and you choose to love Him, that's the place you surrender. And when you've surrendered to a God who loves you, and you love Him, you have trust in Him. These components are all tied together.

The secret place is also the place of *obedience*. A surrendered person—someone who trusts God, someone who has received His love and is loving God and responding to God—will choose to obey God on a daily basis. The fear of the Lord is in you. There's a reverential respect for God. Because God is holy and His holiness comes inside of you, you don't want evil to mix with it, so you purposely avoid and run from evil.

SPEAKING IT OUT

"I will say of the Lord, 'He is my refuge and my fortress; My God, in Him I will trust'" (Ps. 91:2). Because you're dwelling in the secret place, the knowledge that He's your refuge erupts from inside of you. You say, "He's my fortress," because you've been communing with Him. Your trust is in Him because you're relying totally upon Him. Instead of trusting in the casino bingo game, a lottery ticket, the psychic hotline, or the horoscope in the newspaper, begin to say, "My trust is in Him—the Son of God Himself, Jesus Christ." Second Corinthians 4:13 says that the spirit of faith is that we believe, and therefore, we speak. Faith speaks what God has spoken. Every day, say out loud what the Scriptures have promised you. Begin to say, "I will not be afraid...for the Lord my God is with me wherever I go" (see Josh. 1:9).

So often, people declare calamity and tragedy over themselves without even realizing it. If you get in the car with someone who says that they are an accident looking for a place to happen, say, "Excuse me, I'm getting out." Why? You don't want your Psalm 91 going head to head with their confession of death and destruction! We pray before we even get on an airplane. By our faith we anoint those pilots, co-pilots, the air traffic controllers, all the avionics equipment, the engine, and those wheels to go down and come up at the right time, in the Name of Jesus!

One of the most profound stories of someone speaking the Word of God in a terrifying situation is found in the book *Terror at Tenerife.* In 1977, at the airport in Tenerife, Canary Islands, two 747s collided on the runway in foggy weather, fully loaded with both passengers and fuel. When one of the pilots saw the other plane on the runway, he tried to lift off and got just high enough to go right through the top of the other plane. It was tragic because both planes erupted in fire. One of the men who survived said, "When it happened, a ball of fire came right down the passenger area as fuel dumped and exploded right in the main cockpit and started coming down, just burning people alive." He saw that fireball coming straight at him. As he saw it coming, he began to yell, "I'm redeemed by the Blood of the Lamb!" He said it, he looked up, and there was a hole right above him. He was a rather large man, and the area inside of a 747 is almost ten feet to the top of it. But he jumped straight up, grabbed the sides, came off the top, went down on the wing, and jumped off the wing. He had some ankle and leg injuries from jumping from the wing, but he lived to tell how speaking the Word of God delivered his life.[2]

When we begin to declare the Word of God, something happens. Job 22:28 says, "You will also declare a thing, and it will be established for you; so light will shine on your ways." To decree means to order, to decide. You decide that God's promises are going to be what you live by, and you speak those promises with confidence in God's ability and His will. What are you decreeing in your life? Say, "I'm redeemed! I'm blessed! My needs are met! God is my Healer!" Whatever you decree, God will establish it for you. If you're decreeing nothing, then there's nothing for Him to establish. You might say to yourself, "Well, I already know that." That's good that you know it, but until you decree it with your mouth, your faith has not been fully released in that area.

DELIVERED FROM...

Verse 3 of Psalm 91 begins to tell you what you're delivered from: "Surely He shall deliver you from the snare of the fowler and from the perilous pestilence." *Surely* means "absolutely, certainly, you can count on it."[3] The *fowler* is a figurative picture of someone who would catch birds in a trap or a snare. These would be demonic spirits who attempt to arrange wicked plots, traps, snares, or schemes to tempt, test, or destroy a person. God says that He will deliver you from those plans of the enemy. *Perilous pestilence* implies an enemy lying in wait to spoil or rob through a rushing calamity that sweeps over everything before it.

In December, 2005, right before the tsunami hit the coasts of Asia and Africa, a group of Christians in that area wanted to worship on Christmas Day, and they asked permission from the local authorities of the Muslim community to have a large gathering. The authorities told them that they could not have their celebration event in the town but that they could go up to the nearby mountain to celebrate. All of these Christians were high enough in the mountain that when the tsunami came, it did not touch them. God delivered them. God can direct our steps even when we may not fully realize how He is guiding us away from danger.

Psalm 91:4 says, "He shall cover you with His feathers, and under His wings you shall take refuge; His truth shall be your shield and buckler." Here we see the picture of the eagle covering the little eaglets. If you're a little baby eagle, and Momma Eagle is covering you, then you don't have to worry about anything else. No predator is going to try to take on an eagle. *Shield and buckler* refer to weapons of defense. *Buckler* is an Old

English word. The buckler covered the vital organs of the body so that a person would be protected. We know it in the New Testament as the breastplate of righteousness.

YOU WON'T BE AFRAID OF ATTACK

"You shall not be afraid of the terror by night, nor of the arrow that flies by day" (Ps. 91:5). This is very important to take hold of because nightmares, night terrors, and night fear are a terrific plague in our land. Many times people are fearful that they hear noises outside of their apartment or house, or they're afraid of break-ins from intruders. So often evil will happen at night because the works of darkness like to move in that realm. Because you've been given a sound mind (see 2 Tim. 1:7), the darkness of night no longer holds the dread and fear that once bound you. "The arrow that flies by day" would include any missile, projectile, rocket grenade, etc. No bullets are going to strike your body. It doesn't matter how these "arrows" are sent, they will not touch us, and we'll not be afraid of them.

MOTHER AND SON
DELIVERED FROM STRAY BULLETS

A few years ago, when our friend Maria Clinkscales was a single parent, she and her son lived in an apartment next door to a person whom she suspected had people coming often with drugs. Because Maria has been a woman of prayer and has used her faith many times for God's supernatural help, she understood living "in the secret place" of God's presence. She knows the voice of the Holy Spirit. One night she had been in prayer and was praying for others when she felt the Holy Spirit direct her to pray protection over the life of her and her son. Then the Lord said, "When you go to church tomorrow morning, have Pastor Sharon pray over you because there is going to be a shootout in your apartment complex." He also said, "They are not after you and your son, but pray against stray bullets." Maria obeyed what the Lord had told her to do, and Sharon prayed Psalm 91 over Maria and her son. Maria did not know when the shootout would take place, but she followed what the Lord told her to do and then rested in His arms of protection.

The following Saturday, she was the leader of a ladies prayer group at our church building. Her son was in childcare in the church nursery. When she finished the prayer time, she thought she was ready to go home, but the Lord said, "Don't leave yet." She said, "Lord, I'm finished. I've got to go home. I'm hungry, and I have to take care of my son." Again she heard the Lord say, "Don't go yet." So she walked around the building, keeping an attitude of watchfulness and prayer. She knew it probably looked strange for her to just continue walking through the halls when she didn't have any apparent reason to be there, but she knew that she was following the Holy Spirit's leading. Forty-five minutes later, the Holy Spirit said, "It's okay now to go home." So she picked up her son and headed home.

As they pulled up in front of her apartment complex, two police officers walked up to her vehicle and said, "Stay in your car." So they stayed and waited for further instructions. Sometime later the police officers came back and said, "Forty-five minutes ago there was a shootout here and somebody got killed." They asked which apartment was hers, and when she pointed it out, they said that it was between her apartment door and a neighbor's door that the shooting had taken place—during the exact time that she and her son would have been walking to their door if the Lord had not intervened. Because she had been in an attitude of prayer and sensitivity to the Lord, she was in tune with what the Spirit of God was leading her to do. Dwelling in the secret place saved her and her son's lives that day. It will save your life in times of crisis as well.

YOU WON'T BE AFRAID OF DISEASE

Psalm 91 goes on to say that we will not fear "...the pestilence that walks in darkness, nor of the destruction that lays waste at noonday" (Ps. 91:6). A pestilence is a destroying plague. Jesus warned us in Matthew 24:7 that in the last days there would be signs of plagues in different places. We're not afraid of anthrax, bird flu epidemic, *E. coli*, smallpox, AIDS— or any highly infectious disease. Anything that might be fatal is under this category of the destroying plague or pestilence. *Destructions* would include airplanes colliding with buildings, earthquakes, volcanoes, falling meteors, lightning, tidal waves, tsunamis, hurricanes, tornadoes, or floods. We are not going to fear these things.

The passage goes on to say, "A thousand may fall at your side, and ten thousand at your right hand; but it shall not come near you" (Ps. 91:7). What happens around us does not determine our personal safety. Our faith in God and our response to His warnings can determine our safety. God has promised to deliver us.

John G. Lake was a great healing evangelist in the early 1900s. While he served as a missionary in Africa, a plague hit that area, and thousands of people were dying. He began to go minister to them, and people were getting healed. He was asked how he could operate in that area and not be affected. To their amazement, he asked the doctors to take some saliva from someone who had contracted the disease and to put it under a microscope. When they did, they could see the live germs moving around on the slide. He then told them to put the germs on his hand. When they looked at the germs on his hand under the microscope, all of the germs had died. He said it was because of the law of the spirit of life in Christ Jesus. (See Romans 8:2). He wasn't trying to tempt God, but he was demonstrating to them that there was power in knowing Jesus Christ.

When we stand upon this Word, we have an absolute confidence that God is going to direct our steps. When you're in intimate communion with the Lord, part of your deliverance comes because God knows about disastrous things that are ahead, and He's going to lead you another way. If there's ever been an hour when we need to apply this, it is right now. People may ask from time to time, "Well, what do you think about what's going on in the world?" From now on, instead of repeating what the local news media has said, why don't you tell them what the Word of God says? Just use that as an opportunity to say, "Well, you know Psalm 91 says..." and begin to tell it. Wherever you go, God's going with you. We don't worship a God that's far off. As you're in the secret place, He's in the secret place in your heart. You listen to His voice, and He guides you.

NO EVIL WILL BEFALL ME

Psalm 91 goes on to say, "Only with your eyes shall you look, and see the reward of the wicked" (Ps. 91:8). It may be that you will be in places where evil is happening around you. You can trust in this Word that you may see it, but it won't be happening to you. "Because you have made the Lord, who is my refuge, even the Most High, your dwelling place, No evil shall befall you, nor shall any plague come near your dwelling" (Ps. 91:9-10). You need to make it your declaration: "No evil is going to befall us." How much evil? No evil! The words of your mouth are very important in these days and in this hour. Remember, "Death and life are in the power of the tongue" (Prov. 18:21). We will eat the fruit of the words we speak (see Prov. 18:21). People will perish for the lack of knowledge, forgotten knowledge, or knowledge that's failed to be acted upon. (See Hosea 4:6.) Stay in the Bible, and make it your aim to speak what God's Word says instead of what you may see happening around you.

"For He shall give His angels charge over you, to keep you in all your ways. In their hands they shall bear you up, lest you dash your foot against a stone" (Ps. 91:11-12). Your angels are working on your behalf. That word *keep* means "to guard, protect, or deliver you."[6] In what way will He keep you? In *all* of your ways.

"You shall tread upon the lion and the cobra, the young lion and the serpent you shall trample underfoot" (Ps. 91:13). The children of Israel were going into a place where there were lions and snakes, and they would need authority over them. This is also figurative, speaking of our authority over demonic spirits. When a demonic work of the enemy comes against you, instead of it conquering you, you can defeat it. Begin to say, "In the name of Jesus Christ, God has given me power over all the enemy and nothing shall by any means hurt me. I bind the works of darkness, and I loose God's angels to keep me and deliver my life. I give the devil no place. God hasn't given me a spirit of fear but of power, love, and a sound mind." (See Luke 10:19; Matthew 18:18; Ephesians 4:27; and 2 Timothy 1:7).

WHAT GOD WILL DO FOR YOU

Psalm 91 concludes with a powerful list of the benefits of receiving the love of God and responding with love to God. This is what God says of those who set their hearts on Him. Make this Scripture your personal declaration:

Because he has set his love upon Me, therefore I will deliver him; I will set him on high, because he has known My name. He shall call upon Me, and I will answer him; I will be with him in trouble; I will deliver him and honor him. With long life I will satisfy him, and show him My salvation" (Psalm 91:14-16).

People sometimes move away from Psalm 91 simply because they can't explain why something has happened or didn't happen. There are a lot of things about the Lord and about life that you and I may not know, but we still trust God to carry us to the right destination. Don't judge God's faithfulness to His Word because of what Aunt Susie or Grandpa Jones experienced. God is faithful to His Word, and His Word is our final authority. There is no way to know the stand of faith that is in someone else's heart and why they experienced what they did. What is important is to remember that God never fails.

TERRORIST ATTACK
AT U.S. EMBASSY, NAIROBI, KENYA

Glen Wells was unexpectedly called into a meeting on the morning of August 7, 1998, when he was working in the Embassy in Nairobi, Kenya. His mother, Florence, is my personal secretary, and his father, Bill, is one of our board members. Bill and Florence daily quote Psalm 91 over all of their children and have done so for years. Glen wrote this account of his experience:

My day started out like any other day in Nairobi, Kenya. It was August 7, 1998. I was working in the U.S. Embassy there. At about 9:30, my boss asked me to attend a weekly meeting at 10:00 in the Ambassador's Office in his place, as he had something else to do. [Glen had to leave his office to go to this meeting.] Little did I know that, at that same time, agents of Osama bin Laden were on the other side of the town making final preparations for an attack on our Embassy. It was to be a bold strike by the terrorist genius—a simultaneous attack on two Embassies in East Africa—Nairobi and Dar es Salaam, Tanzania. Before 9/11, this type of coordination by terrorists was unheard of.

Shortly after 10:30, three men in a small truck laden with explosives pulled up to the back of the Embassy and attempted to make their way into the underground Embassy parking garage. If they had been able to set off their bomb inside the garage, the Embassy itself would have been transformed into a large explosive and would surely have come toppling down on itself, destroying much of downtown Nairobi.

The terrorists' plan faltered, however, when one terrorist, whose role was to jump out of the vehicle and place a gun to the head of the Embassy guards—left his weapon in his coat, which he had left in the vehicle. When the guards refused to open the gate, the terrorist reached for the grenade and threw it and then fled. The other terrorists in the vehicle apparently saw no other recourse but to set off the bomb in the parking lot.

Meanwhile, in the Ambassador's Office, we heard the grenade go off and then eight seconds later, the loudest sound I have ever heard. It shook the building. Windows were blown out; all electricity was immediately cut. Senior officers started barking orders to vacate the building via the stairs. Not seeing any of my colleagues, however, I made my way back to my office. As I inched my way through the debris-cluttered darkened hallway, I could hear the screams of pain of our secretary. And then as I turned the corner, I could see outside lights shining through where a wall used to be. I realized the extent of the attack. All offices along the back side of the Embassy and some interior offices had been destroyed, including mine. Many Embassy colleagues—many of whom had gone to the window following the grenade explosion—had either been killed or were severely injured lying under mounds of debris.

I helped carry a colleague who had been severely wounded in his face and was virtually unrecognizable, and I placed him in an Embassy vehicle headed to the hospital. I found another wounded colleague shortly thereafter. And as we were driving to the hospital, he started telling me how he had not been living for God and how he needed to get his life right with God. We prayed right there as we sped along madly through the streets of Nairobi. I grabbed a bunch of Gideon Testaments from the back of my car, and I spent the rest of the day searching for and praying with my wounded colleagues.

The blast killed over 200 people and wounded over 5,000, the vast majority of whom were innocent Kenyans. Although the Embassy structure survived the explosion, a nearby seven-story office building housing a secretarial school in the middle of class—it fell to the ground like a deck of cards. Another thirty-story building showered broken glass on passers by. Buses and vehicles, waiting in Nairobi's infamous traffic jams, and their passengers were immediately incinerated.

One of the most miraculous stories to come out of this horrible event was the story of the Embassy guards who refused to raise the gate. Four out of the five walked away without any injuries from the site. You see, the grenade blast had knocked them all to the ground, and when the major explosion went off, it passed right over them. It doesn't matter where you are, you can be next to a megaton bomb, but the safest place to be is right in the middle of the will of God.[7]

That's where Glen was–right in the middle of the will of God. As a result of his steps being ordered of the Lord, Glen was put in a position to save others that day. Looking back on the incident, Glen wasn't supposed to be in that meeting in another office on that day. His boss asked him to go in his place. When you are speaking the Word of God over yourself on a regular basis, you will find that what the world calls "coincidence" is really the hand of God moving you out of harm's way. Your steps are being ordered more than you realize it. Keep your eyes on His Word and just keep walking.

ENDNOTES

1. Finnis Jennings Dake, *The Dake Annotated Reference Bible* (Lawrenceville, GA: Dake Publishing, 1999), s.v. "Yashab."
2. Norman Williams and George Otis, *Terror at Tenerife: The Canary Islands Crash* (Van Nuys, CA: Bible Voice, 1977).
3. *Dake*, s.v. "Surely."

Chapter 12

KEEP YOUR FOCUS

We like to go fishing. It's something we grew up doing as a pastime and we still enjoy it. If you've ever been fishing, you know how important it is to get to that exact place where the fish are located. You motor out there and get right to that spot. You don't want to drop the anchor and scare the fish, so you and that boat just sit in the water and cast your line. There may be a slight breeze blowing across the pond or lake, and as you sit there for a few minutes, you realize that you are not where you were originally. That breeze was blowing ever so slightly, imperceptible to the eye. If you were looking at the water, you might have seen just a little ripple in your line to indicate that you were moving. But if you're focused on a tree or a land marker, you realize that you were moving across the lake the whole time. You didn't decide to move. It wasn't your desire to be in a different spot than where you began. You didn't say, "I'm just getting away from where these fish are biting." No, you were *drifting* because there was no anchor to hold you in place.

If we don't turn our thoughts and conversations back to the Word of God and His benefits, it's possible to begin to *drift* away from the truth. Hebrews 2:1 reminds us to "give the more earnest heed to the things we have heard, lest we drift away." In other words, pay close attention to the Word that you've learned in your walk with Christ so that you don't find yourself believing and thinking what's contrary to the Word. There are people who are in drift. They love God. You may ask them, "Do you believe in Jesus?" They say, "Oh, yes, I'm a believer in Jesus." But where they are right now is not where they used to be. Some used to be on fire for the Lord, studying the Word of God on a daily basis. They had an intensity, at one time, for the things of God, but they didn't have an anchor to keep them in that place. Maybe their job changed and they weren't able to be at church on a regular basis, or maybe the lake was calling them on Sunday morning and they took the lake's call and put God on hold. After a period of weeks, months, or years, one day they looked up and realized they were no longer where they were supposed to be.

When September 11, 2001, came, suddenly every church in America had a marked increase in attendance. The boost wasn't necessarily from the unsaved, un-churched people either. We had a huge jump in our own church in the days and weeks after 9/11, and we were grateful that they knew to come to church at a time like that. But why weren't they there before? They had drifted away from church, and suddenly a calamity made them realize "That's where I need to be. That's what's important." Some continued in church attendance after that, but some slipped back into a distant place in their relationship to God.

In these past years, more and more distractions have been keeping people preoccupied with other activities and keeping them away from God and the Church. Many things are now happening on Sundays. Sports have increased their activities on Sunday like never before. It used to be that there was no sport that happened with young people on Sunday, but today there are many games, conferences, rallies, and tournaments that are held over a weekend, robbing families of being at their local church. Parents have begun to bow down to the god of sports; they worship it. In the Old Testament they worshipped Baal, "the lord of the flies." In America we have *baals* today that people worship—basket-*baal*, foot-*baal*, soccer-*baal*. Parents will say, "Well, it's very important to my child to be at this event. They may get a trophy or a scholarship." Yes, their participation might get them an award or scholarship, but if this becomes a habit in their lives—putting everything else ahead of God—you'll reap children who don't reverence and respect God. Are sports events worth the consequences of drifting from church attendance? Understand that when people lose reverence and respect for God, they also lose moral boundaries and respect for their parents and others.

It's my prayer that we would not have to have a calamity to get us back on target and that we would focus on what's important, whether the economy is up or down, whether we're at peace or at war. Drop your anchor into the water of God's Word and let it keep you secure in the times ahead. Fellowshipping with other believers and getting into a solid, Word-based church will strengthen your walk. The winds of fear and reason will try to blow against all of us from time to time, but when your focus is on the Word of God, you will stand through it all.

THIS GREAT SALVATION

Have you considered recently the benefits of salvation that you have received? If you've been in the church awhile, sometimes that zeal and excitement can wear off. A Word from God, a prophecy, or the inner witness inside of our hearts becomes mundane and expected. No longer does Jesus' sacrifice have the same place in hearts as it once did. Yes, some people are "saved," but they've neglected to grow any further than the last Word that they heard from God because they're not putting Jesus and His Kingdom first.

In the social services world, neglect is a very serious issue. It's a tragedy when we hear of parents neglecting their children's needs. What happens to the child who is neglected? The child usually functions below the normal standard of other children the same age. I'm not talking about those who can't afford to provide. On the contrary, neglect has to do with seeing a need and ignoring it—whether it's physical, emotional, or spiritual. When it comes to machinery, public services, and things that we as a society depend on, neglect could not only cause many to suffer but it could also cost people's lives. Wake up! Don't neglect your relationship with God.

God has warned us about neglecting the life that salvation has wrought for us. In Hebrews 2:2-3, He says:

For if the word spoken through angels proved steadfast, and every transgression and disobedience received a just reward, how shall we escape if we neglect so great a salvation, which at the first began to be spoken by the Lord, and was confirmed to us by those who heard Him (Hebrews 2:2-3).

By definition *neglect* means to "not care for something properly; fail to do something."[1] So why does not properly caring for our salvation affect the thoughts of fear and terror rushing through our minds? If you neglect a garden, the weeds will overrun it. You have to give attention to a garden to keep the weeds out and to make sure that there's water on the plants. If you neglect a car and don't change the oil in it for five years, it would probably destroy the engine. If you neglect your salvation, emptiness comes. Out of emptiness comes deception. The devil will give you another offer to fill up that emptiness, and out of that offer comes destruction. That's when many people enter depression.

When the angels spoke and people neglected it, they were penalized. But we're in a whole different ballpark. *God* is the One who spoke to us with signs, wonders, and miracles. We are to give importance to the things we have heard, lest we drift away. I would say this is serious business. Hebrews 12:25 says, "See that you do not refuse Him that is speaking to you...." Don't ignore His promptings. Listen to Him and obey Him.

Neglect and drift go together. Drift happens without even perceiving it. Neglect is not something you set out to do; it's just a process. The Bible asks, *"How will we escape..."* (Heb. 2:3). Begin to soak and saturate yourself with the Word of God. He is your Prince of Peace, your Deliverer, and your Provider. This is not the time to be saturated with what the world is saying. It's our time to be wrapped up in our great salvation and to stay free from fear.

SALVATION'S BENEFITS

When you start a new job, you want to know about the benefits right away. You come home and tell your wife or husband all that your employer is providing. Not only do you get paid to do your job and earn a salary, but they may be providing some form of health, dental, and life insurance benefits to top it off. You tell your friends and maybe your close neighbors about this great job that you landed and all that's provided for you and your family.

Now let's talk about your new benefits of salvation—some you probably didn't even realize you had. In salvation, your grace benefits begin with the forgiveness of your sins. You're no longer unclean; you are now righteous. When you're right with God, then you can have the peace *of* God, peace *with* God, and peace with others. But that's just the beginning. You've even been given a new residence as a benefit. Instead of being headed to hell, you're now on the road to Heaven. Your earthly family may have been dysfunctional; your heavenly family is not. You may have experienced a horrible problem. You may have been abused, rejected, compared, or criticized as a child, but your heavenly Father loves you with a perfect love. You have a Savior who was willing to give His blood, to die in your place, and He is ever interceding (praying) for you right now at the right hand of the Father. His prayers always get through. Add to that Colossians 1:13, which says, "He has delivered us from the power of darkness and conveyed us into the kingdom of the Son of His love." You mean I don't have to be doing the same sin I was doing before? That's right. You've been placed or moved into a new Kingdom. Sin is no longer your nature; by faith you walk out of sin and into living right. You can share that with your relatives. What a deal!

How about the material provisions for you and your family, such as clothing, food, and shelter? Matthew 6:33 tells us exactly how to get these: Seek God and His righteousness first and He'll just add those to you. That's like working for an employer who says, "You meet with me every day and go where I send you. I'll tell you what I'll do then. I'll just start sending shipments of whatever you need directly to your house. It's not part of your salary either. Because you're putting my business first, I just want to do that for you." You may think, *That sounds too good to be true.* When you decided to live for God, He said that's the way it will work. But what about the healing of this ailment or disease? God says, "I've already got that covered. Jesus took the whippings on His back so that you can be healed." First Peter 2:24 says, "...by whose stripes you were healed."

Can anything separate us from the love of God? Could demonic spirits, hard times, or a bad season separate us from that love. No! Romans 8:37 tells us that none of that can stop us, for "we are more than conquerors through Him who loved us." And with everything that happens around us, we rely on Romans 8:28 to see us through: "And we know that all things work together for good to those who love God, to those who are the called according to His purpose." We even project that thought into our future by saying, "Father, my faith is that everything ahead of me is working together for good."

There are many more Scriptures that talk about the benefits of salvation. The next time someone wants to tell you the latest threat they heard on the evening news, tell them, "Hey,

I've got something good for you," and then tell them about the blessings of being in the Kingdom of God. It may surprise them that you could change the conversation around so quickly, but it is exactly what both of you need.

WHAT DID YOU SAY?

Whatever you talk about, you appreciate. Whatever you think on and magnify gets bigger in your mind. And like a magnet, whatever you're thinking and talking about is attracted to you—whether it's good or bad. It's time to change your focus. What are you talking about? The terror alerts and threats or what God is doing in the earth? You can focus on either one. One will keep you in captivity; the other will liberate you.

I want to encourage you to talk about the greatness of God. Our God is performing miracles daily. Revival is happening in churches and cities all over the world. God is not in a box. He's moving and bringing salvation on an hourly, daily, weekly, monthly basis. Our world is ripe for more revival, without a doubt, but God is not limited to our finite minds. He is a now God who is constantly on the move. What happened yesterday in your church can be inspiring, but what He's about to do will totally take you by surprise. Revivals of the past are wonderful to study and learn from, but don't think that that's the end of His power in the earth. The best is yet to come.

When we've held large evangelistic meetings in Dominican Republic, Haiti, or Russia, we've seen deaf ears opened, blind eyes receive sight, and the crippled begin to walk. We've witnessed demonic spirits cast out as never before. One girl that came to one of our meetings in the Dominican Republic was so possessed by demons that she was kicking and screaming violently, unable to be still. Some of our youth who went with us on the trip were standing close to this girl, and they began to pray for her. They commanded the devils to leave her in the name of Jesus. She was gloriously saved and set free on the same night. In fact, we found out that she had been normal until a few months before the crusade. Her mother took her to doctors and no one could help her. Her mother, who was also unsaved, brought her to our meeting because she heard that miracles were happening there. That night, when the daughter was delivered, she and her mother were both saved.

The next evening, as we called for testimonies of healings, a young teenager accompanied to the platform a young woman who had received healing when we prayed over the people. She wanted to testify to what the Lord had done. We realized that the young teenager who was leading the other young woman to the platform was the same one from the night before who had been set free from demons. We didn't even recognize her! She was in her right mind and was a beautiful girl. God had so touched her life and set her free that when people raised their hands to be healed, she laid her hands on the young woman next to her, and that young woman was healed in her ear that had gone deaf. That night we all celebrated that both of these girls had been saved and healed.

Some people teach that these kinds of miracles were done away with after the first century apostles died. I don't find anywhere in my Bible evidence that God put a time limit on His miracles. It's a good thing—because with all of the miracles we see, we'd be in complete violation of that commandment! Jesus told us to do these acts in Mark 16:15-18, and I believe it.

These miracles are not happening only overseas in Third World countries, but we regularly see these same signs and wonders in our own church services. We have had instances of people being healed while Sharon sings, with no one even touching the people: the insane having their right mind restored, those in wheelchairs beginning to take steps, and those brought in on stretchers leaving the service on two feet. People are being healed of cancer, diabetes, depression, and various other ailments. God is moving among His people, and He has never stopped.

Psalm 96:3 says, "Declare His glory among the nations, His wonders among all peoples." Renew your mind and inspire your spirit with books, tapes, and videos about God's supernatural workings. Get your "expecter" ready to work, and look for the glory of God to be revealed in your church, your city, and your nation. No matter what it looks like around you, God is working behind the scenes.

ENDNOTE

1. *MSN Encarta Dictionary,* s.v. "Neglect," http://encarta.msn.com/encnet/features/dictionary/dictionaryhome.aspx.

Chapter 13

DON'T FEED FEAR!

When it comes to staying free from fear, we have to watch what we're putting into ourselves. If you want to walk in faith, take inventory of what you're watching, listening to, and allowing in your spirit. Some folks are addicted to bad news. They thrive on watching and listening to all the bad news that they can. They can recite all of the murders that happened this week—where they happened, how they happened, and who they think committed them. The murder television series have become particularly popular in the last few years. People watch them and say, "It's so interesting. They're going to find out who did it." In the meantime, the spirit of fear is coming on them as they're thinking about the whole process of murder. You can't watch shows like that without being affected.

There are others who thrive on watching spooky movies. I told Sharon when I first started dating her, "There are a couple of things I don't do. I don't ride roller coasters, and I don't watch spooky movies." Now Sharon had to get delivered from watching scary movies. As a youngster, she and her brother would watch them, and when she went to bed at night, she'd wear a cross necklace to combat the fear. Because of the scary movies she had watched, she thought that wearing that cross would take care of everything. However, she still had thoughts of fear that would bother her. One day her mom said, "If watching scary programs affects you like that, quit watching them." That was the encouragement she needed. Every now and then, she would watch an old movie that would cause those fears to rise again. Then one day, we began to hear people teach on meditating and confessing the Word of God. We began to memorize Scriptures on protection, peace, authority, and other areas. That Word changed Sharon's and my way of thinking. Faith began to dominate our thoughts.

You're bound to hear of terror threats and calamities in the earth, but work to limit how much you allow yourself to hear. Turn off the television or radio if necessary. Feed your mind with worship music and good teaching materials that can increase your faith and your children's faith. Your words have control over your thoughts, so take the Word of God and literally shove the negative thoughts out of your mind.

FEED YOUR CHILDREN WORDS OF FAITH

Psychologists cautioned parents after 9/11 to guard their children from repeatedly seeing the video footage of the collapse of the Towers. It put negative images in people's minds, especially the minds of innocent children who could hardly grasp that there are evil people in the world who would harm other human beings. It can make them feel vulnerable to satan's attacks. Children are like sponges, soaking up whatever is around them. If you want faith in them instead of fear, you have to be the one to put it in their minds and hearts. Choose carefully the television shows, documentaries, video games, Internet pages, music on their iPod, and movies that your children see and hear, and use wisdom about how often they should be allowed to watch or listen to them. Many people want to warn their children about avoiding dangerous situations, so they tell them scary, spooky stories to illustrate their point. Then the children have nightmares because of what they were told.

There is a way to warn and guide children without putting a spirit of fear inside of them. Putting faith and obedience in their hearts through the Word of God is much more productive. In Isaiah 54:13, the Lord says, "All of your children shall be taught by the Lord, and great shall be the peace of your children." This is a promise you need to stand on and speak over your children: "My children are taught by the Lord, and great is the peace of my children." Parents and guardians are the primary teachers of God's Word to children. We thank God for Sunday school, children's church, youth ministry, and Christian school, but the parent is the one who is assigned to be with the children and instruct them. Many people want to abdicate that responsibility and release it to someone else. If anything goes wrong with their child, they blame everyone else. The Church is called alongside to help you, but it is your responsibility and your calling to raise up your children to know and obey the voice of God.

Instead of the negative, fear-filled television shows that many are watching, Philippians 4:8 gives us some direction about what we are to feed our minds:

Finally, brethren, whatever things are true, whatever things are noble, whatever things are just, whatever things are pure, whatever things are lovely, whatever things are of good report, if there is any virtue and if there is anything praiseworthy—meditate on these things.

You might have to search a while at the video rental places or the theater to find movies or shows that have these attributes, but they are out there. If your children hear of terror situations and share their concern with you, open up the Word of God and help shed some light on the subject. Both you and your children will be encouraged in faith to stop the spirit of fear.

A BALANCED LOOK AT PROPHETIC EVENTS

There is a big difference between being informed and being terrified. Many well-meaning ministers paint a grim picture of end-time prophetic events. It causes torment in people because they are not aware of God's purpose in foretelling the events. Luke 21:26 warns that when people get a large dose of only the negative aspects of life and feed on thoughts of doom and gloom, then their hearts will fail them from fear because of what they see happening on the earth.

I don't deny that we live in perilous times or the fact that Scriptures concerning this period of time are coming to pass on what seems like a daily basis. The Word of God is very clear concerning the end of time as we know it. However, as Jesus was foretelling these prophetic events, He encouraged his disciples: "Then they will see the Son of Man coming in a cloud with power and great glory. Now when these things begin to happen, look up and lift up your heads, because your redemption draws near" (Luke 21:27-28). Jesus is returning some day, and I believe that day is soon. So I choose to meditate on what I'm supposed to be doing until He returns. I stay informed about current events, especially as they relate to biblical prophecy, but I don't let those events determine my peace and joy in this world. My peace and joy are wrapped up in Jesus, and He will see me through whatever He calls me to do and wherever He calls me to go.

Keeping our minds on Him and His will for our lives will cause peace to reign and guard our hearts and thoughts. Isaiah 26:3 says, "You will keep him in perfect peace, whose mind is stayed on You, because he trusts in You." Jesus said concerning the end-time events, "These things I have spoken to you, that in Me you may have peace. In the world you will have tribulation; but be of good cheer, I have overcome the world" (John 16:33). Jesus has overcome all the power of this world. You can have peace and joy in the midst of crisis around you as you turn to the Prince of Peace. He sets you free for a purpose, so go on and fulfill His awesome plan for your life.

Chapter 14

WALKING INTO
YOUR PURPOSE

Fear and terror had a purpose in your life. They possibly caused you to pull back, hide, and cower. They may have even caused you to change your course, and they may have kept you in the back corner of despair. But now they've been identified and forced out of the dark shadows. They've come to the light of His presence and were found as liars and deceivers with no truth in them. What the devil meant to harm you is going to turn for your good. No longer a prisoner, you've been supernaturally freed from bondage and given seasoned weapons to become the warrior that you were meant to be. God's love is now permeating your being. His creative, awesome intellect has fashioned you to fulfill your purpose in this world. He's not mad at you. On the contrary, He loves you. You've been created by the Master Craftsman to show the world His handiwork in human form. There is no higher creation than humanity, and you are a treasured possession that He has written on the palm of His hand. Nothing can hold you back now.

But is this newfound freedom given to us just so that we can enjoy life and carry on business as usual? Is it strictly for our benefit that He has demolished the strongholds of satan? Could there be a higher purpose than what we've known or understood?

WHAT'S MY PURPOSE?

I graduated from college with a bachelor's degree, with minor in physical education and a major in Christian education. As one of my good friends told me, about the best thing I could do with that degree was become a church league basketball coach. But God had His plans. My calling to become a pastor didn't occur to me until after I had graduated and become involved with ministry. Sharon and I had worked with young people, leading church camps and summer youth groups. We enjoyed relating to teens, so when an opportunity to work as a youth pastor at a local church came up, I applied for it. I didn't hear back from the senior pastor for awhile after I had made application. When two other out-of-state job offers came, I turned them down. I decided to call back the pastor and see if the job was still open before we left Tulsa after my graduation from Oral Roberts University in May, 1974.

I found out the position was still unfilled. With hesitation the pastor sighed and said, "Why don't we try you out for three months. If we like you and you like us at that point, you can stay on." It was not exactly a resounding confirmation of approval, but it was a job that I felt we were called to and wanted to do, so we took it. During that probation period, the youth group grew dramatically. We went from about 14 kids to close to 100. God gave us ideas to minister to the youth through different outreaches. It was an amazing time. We liked them, and they liked us, so we stayed on.

One time, not really knowing what our next step would be, I was sitting in a service at the church while Kenneth Copeland was ministering. I was just sitting as a member of the congregation when I heard inside of my heart, "You will be the next pastor of this church." The fulfillment of this word wouldn't take place until nearly four years later. We were in our early twenties, and I knew not to tell anyone this word that we had heard from the Lord. We were directed by the Lord to travel in ministry for two years and eight months before we returned to ministry at this church. Soon after our return, we were asked to be pastors of the church in 1979 and God began to fulfill His word that He had spoken to us. Let me say that not everyone is called to the pulpit ministry. God calls people to be coaches, teachers, business people, scientists, and myriads of other professions. There is no shortage of the kinds of occupations and callings that He has placed inside human beings. For as many people that He has created, He has something for each one of us to do.

STEPPING INTO YOUR CALLING

I'm a strong proponent of higher education and have gone on to receive a master's and a doctorate degree, as well as Bible school training, but as my life can attest, a calling is more than just education. It has to do with God's call on our lives above all. Just as an architect draws up plans for a new building, God, the Master Architect, has a master plan that He wants carried out on this earth. It's perfectly drawn to scale; the dimensions are exact, and the directions are clear. You and I were created to be the trusted members of the construction crew to do our part to build His plan in the earth. Luke 19:10 tells us God's purpose for sending Jesus to the earth: "To seek and to save that which was lost." Thank God, that included you and me. But it also includes your neighbors, co-workers, and relatives. God is building His Kingdom through you and me.

That's why He continually tells us, "Fear not!" If you have fear, you'll stop in your tracks. You'll think that your purposes are more important than His. But when you know that you were saved for a purpose—to finish the work that Jesus started and left for us to do—then it makes sense. His plan was never just to heap the blessing on us so that we could do whatever *we* wanted to do. No, it was so that we could be ready and willing at a moment's notice to go where He sends, say what He says, and ultimately bring people back into fellowship with Him. That's why we can travel where He says without fear of danger.

The first time we were in Sierra Leone, West Africa, to hold a crusade, the country was in the middle of a civil war. Rebel soldiers would shoot a hard drug into their bodies, and then they would just go wild and start slaughtering whole villages. Many innocent people had their limbs chopped off because of these crazed rebels. The city where we held the crusade was in Bo, which was about fifty miles from the rebel base. They did- n't tell me how close we were to the rebel base until a couple of days into the crusade. I'll never forget when they finally told me. The thought came to me, *They've invaded other villages and towns. They can do the same thing here.*

But at night and throughout the day, we would speak Scriptures of God's protection over us, and it routed out the spirit of fear from all of us on the team. We had complete peace. Some time later, we went back to hold a crusade in the city that was held by the rebels. By this time, they had laid down their weapons and surrendered to the governing authorities. God put it in our hearts to go and minister to the people in that city because they had terrorized the people in this area and there was great need for the Gospel. We knew that many of the rebels were still there. When they laid down their weapons, the country granted many of them amnesty and didn't imprison them. We were right in the middle of it. But the spirit of fear never got on us or our team because we continued to believe that God was with us and that He would help us minister to the people.

One of the young men who helped us had watched the rebels kill his family and had part of his arm and his hand cut off. He had escaped and ended up going to Bible school. After he graduated, he shared that one day he came face to face with the man who had killed his family and maimed him. The man was afraid when he saw him. This young, strong, Christian Bible school graduate stood and told the murderer, "I forgive you and I want to share with you how Jesus Christ can change your life." He led the man to the Lord as the man cried out for forgiveness and salvation. God has used this young man to minister to many in his nation because he accepted the call of God upon his life.

This same calling applies to every occupation. If you're a coach, be a soul-winner; if you're a teacher, be a soul-winner; if you're a dentist, a secretary, or a factory-worker, be a soul-winner. God didn't just give you a job so that you could succeed for yourself. Some people say, "Well, business is business and church is church. Don't mix the two." Don't fall for that lie. As a believer, your work should honor God in all ways, but it should also be a conduit to bring people into the Kingdom of God. In whatever field God has placed you or whatever education and experience He has given you—He has had only one goal in mind: to make you more like Him and help you fulfill His calling. When fear is removed from our lives, it's time to fill that place with the purposes of God. It's time to win the lost for His glory. Fear has stopped you from doing this in the past through isolation.

As I've said before, fear and terror paralyze people. They look inward for some feeling of safety, and they continue to stay to themselves. Fear isolates people and shuts them down from reaching out to those around them. If a doctor's report comes back and indicates that a person has six weeks to live, the devil through fear wants this individual to stop building the Kingdom and to begin making plans for the end of his or her days on this earth. No longer is Kingdom business a top priority because preoccupation with death shakes this person to the depths of his or her soul. But we have a Kingdom that cannot be shaken. As Hebrews 12:28 says, "Therefore, since we are receiving a kingdom which cannot be shaken, let us have grace, by which we may serve God acceptably with reverence and godly fear." With God's grace, we'll be His workmen and work the harvest of souls that He has assigned to us. Make plans to live and finish your course on the earth. We have purpose and calling. We have freedom and wisdom. Let us link arms together and keep following our Leader. Jesus can be trusted. When the world around us seems to have the upper hand through terror, we can know that God has equipped us to combat fear in order to ultimately accomplish His goals on the earth.

Chapter 15

YOUR WEAPONS FOR FIGHTING FEAR

God has not made us defenseless in this world. We don't throw stones or use guns to make our point, nor do we sit back and take whatever is aimed at us. Our artillery is not seen with the naked eye, but it is more powerful than any weapon out there. When we take out those God-given weapons, shine them up, and clean them out, we have been known to completely change situations and annihilate the plans of the enemy against our lives. God tells us in Ephesians 6:11 that in order to fight this enemy, we have to put on all of the armor. Don't leave some of it at home and then wonder why the battle isn't going in your favor. This isn't a schoolyard fight that everybody goes home from and all is okay the next day. No, this is serious business that you need to be aware is coming at you.

When members of our military wear their uniforms in a foreign land, they become instant targets of the enemy. They may have absolutely nothing to do with foreign policy decisions or actual combat. They're just following their commanding officer's orders. They might be part of the ancillary services of a cook or a chaplain who is there to help support the armed services. But because they're wearing that uniform, the enemy looks at them as a potential target.

As a Christian, you are now wearing the armor of God, a uniform that is very obvious to the devil. You may not want to be in combat; you may just rather get your ticket punched for Heaven and be done with it. But God has work for you to do, He has enabled you to do it, and He has made provision for you to win. The very fact that His Blood has purchased you makes you an instant recipient of the enemy's "mortar" attacks. So it would be wise for you to understand how to wear the armor that God has given you so that you can win the battles that are raging around you. All warriors have to learn how to wear their armor and how to use their weapons. That's why boot camp is so essential. Our country doesn't just send out young men and women to the front lines who have never had experience handling weapons. Sometimes that six-week training is all they get before they're shipped out, but nevertheless, they better be ready for the enemy, because the enemy is ready for them.

THE BELT OF TRUTH

Your first piece of armor is the *belt of truth* (see Eph. 6:14). Around a soldier's waist is his belt to hold his uniform in place. As a battle is raging, a belt can hold bullets and ammunition easier, providing quicker access than a knapsack behind them. Soldiers have to be able to re-fire as quickly as possible if they want to win the battle. The Word of God is truth (see John 17:17). When you're in a battle with fear, you don't have time to sit down with your Bible in your recliner, sip your coffee or tea, and casually do a Word study about the subject of fear or terror. If you've ever been through a situation that caused your world to rock and shake, you know that you have to have something on the inside of you to combat the thoughts and feelings that you're experiencing. What comes out of your mouth is crucial at those times.

We faced a battle for our daughter Ruthie's life when she was a baby. She was not gaining weight as she should have been, so the doctor suggested that Sharon stop breastfeeding and put her on the bottle so that we could measure exactly how much milk she was taking in. When Sharon took her in to the doctor for her next checkup, Ruthie was six months old and weighed only twelve pounds. The doctor recognized there was an infection in her body, so he prescribed an antibiotic for Sharon to get at the store on her way home. However, as she was leaving the doctor's office, he felt that he should get a blood-count check on Ruthie. The Christian doctor said to her, "As a doctor, this is what my training and skill must report to you. The diagnosis could be spinal meningitis, a rare type of pneumonia, or leukemia, but I believe that by the stripes of Jesus, she is healed" (see Is. 53:5). We were thankful for a Christian doctor. However, Ruthie had several doctors. Some were not as positive. We kept our conversation and faith focused on the Word of God. God uses doctors and nurses, medicines, and tests, but our source of hope is in the Word of God. It is the final authority in our lives.

Sharon and I had studied and memorized Scriptures about healing. For months, we kept our words in line with the Word of God, the truth, and spoke over her only what the Word of God said concerning healing. The tests for spinal meningitis and pneumonia immediately came back negative, praise God! But Ruthie was still not gaining weight and was disinterested in eating. Her white blood cell count began to go down, but it still remained in the 20,000 realm; a normal white blood cell count for a baby is 3,500 to 10,400. She didn't have an appetite, so we had to force her to eat or take a bottle. It was a very serious situation.

We continued to speak the words of truth that had gotten down deep inside of us. Because we didn't want negative words spoken about her, we told only a few people who would stand in faith with us and pray Scriptures regarding her life. During that time, a guest evangelist, who came to speak at our church, went to lunch with us. Sarah, who was two at the time, and Ruthie also came with us. We didn't tell the evangelist anything about Ruthie, but she looked over at her and said, "I want to pray over Ruthie. The Lord showed me to lay hands on her and pray. God is turning this sickness today. In two weeks' time she will begin to be hungry and want to eat, and the day will come when she will out-eat Sarah." At the time, Sarah was a stocky, healthy toddler and a good eater. The evangelist's words to us were confirmation of what we had been speaking over Ruthie.

One day, in about two weeks' time, Ruthie awakened with an appetite. She was so hungry and wanted to eat. She began gaining weight and continued to develop normally, both physically and mentally. Within eleven months, Ruthie's blood count was normal. Her growth was normal, too. There was no sign of leukemia or any other disease. Today she is married and is healthy and whole. God has used her and her husband, Adam, to pray for others and to release healing miracles. We know that the words of truth concerning healing that we had stored in us before Ruth became sick had much to do with the successful outcome of that battle.

Don't wait for an illness or a major setback to get into the Word of God. Continually take time to hear the Word and begin to put into practice what you hear. Begin to stand in faith for healing and health. There are healing Scriptures at the back of this book as a beginning study in that area.

THE BREASTPLATE OF RIGHTEOUSNESS

The next piece of armor that we should be wearing is the *breastplate of righteousness*. A breastplate would be located over a soldier's chest and would guard his heart and vital internal organs. It was usually made of a heavy metal that would be difficult for bullets to penetrate. As a Christian, your righteousness is like a bullet-proof vest against the enemy's devices. He's out to steal your standing with God, trying to make you feel like yesterday's mistake or sin is your complete downfall. He tries to pick at that piece of armor until you just want to take it off and lay it aside. Feelings of unworthiness and failure overwhelm you to the point that you just want to quit the fight. Don't fall for that tactic of the enemy. First John 1:9 is your defense, "If we confess our sins, He is faithful and just to forgive us our sins and to cleanse us from all unrighteousness." You overcome the enemy's accusations when you take by faith Christ's righteousness and stand strong once again. Knowing that you have received righteousness through your faith in Jesus Christ allows you to "come boldly to the throne of God's grace without fear in order to receive His mercy and His help in your time of need" (Heb. 4:16).[1]

YOUR FOOT GEAR

Soldiers can't afford to take much time off to nurse minor wounds, much less to nurse ridiculous injuries, like stepping on a rock. That's why, even when the battle takes place in a hot, sun-scorched desert, you won't find soldiers in sandals. What you will find on their feet are toe-enclosed, solid, lace-up boots with heavy tread for protection. This way, they will have appropriate covering for their feet so that they can get to wherever the battle is raging and endure. Whether they're in the jungle, in the desert, or on a smooth plain, their feet have to be protected.

The third part of your armor against the enemy also comes in the form of foot covering. It says in Ephesians 6:15 that we are to "shod [our] feet with the preparation of the gospel of peace." The word *shod* is another form of the word *shoe*.[2] The "preparation of the gospel of peace" has to do with being prepared to preach the good news in whatever location we find ourselves. The "good news" is that Jesus died, was resurrected, and ascended into Heaven so that people who believe can be saved, delivered, healed, and given newness of life. Are you prepared to share your faith at the drop of a hat? If you are asked for the hope that is within you, could you boldly tell others about your Savior? This is part of your armor against the enemy. If he can shut down your message, he has stopped you in your tracks. You won't advance further against him because you will be "shoe-less." Many Christians never seek to know the Scriptures in order to share them with others. Can you rightly handle the Word of Truth in order to help others understand (see 2 Tim. 2:15)? Taking time daily for reading, studying, and memorizing Scripture will enable you to speak with more assurance and knowledge with others. Ask the Holy Spirit to anoint your words and mannerisms as you share with others to convince them of the truth.

Do you need to put on your boots or have them re-tread? Practice walking in your boots by sharing your faith with others on a regular basis. That way you can advance in the battle and not retreat from the enemy. You're prepared to give others the same drink of water that set you free. Begin to say, "I am ready always to give an answer to every man or woman who asks me a reason for the hope that is in me" (see 1 Pet. 3:15).

THE SHIELD OF FAITH

"Above all," according to Ephesians 6:16, we should take "the shield of faith with which you will be able to quench all the fiery darts of the wicked one." That means that, more than any of the weapons that I've told you about so far, you don't want to leave out this weapon. The shield for soldiers was the first layer of defense in their armor. They would hold up that shield to deflect the arrows of the enemy before they reached their bodies. The shield was sometimes almost as large as the man himself. For Christians, the faith shield that we use in combat comes from hearing the Word of God (see Rom. 10:17). Another way to say that is that we must continually hear the Word of God. Don't just hear it on Sundays or at a mid-week service. Hear yourself saying it out loud as you read or pray Scriptures. It builds a knowing in your heart that it is true, and it enables you with the power to stand against any adversary or terror situation.

I had a miraculous experience in the early years of our ministry that required a strong shield of faith to make it through. I wanted to get my pilot's license so that I could minister wherever and whenever the Lord wanted me to. I began to take flying lessons, but I didn't take lessons long enough to earn my instrument rating. Nevertheless, flying solo was a dream come true! My high school was having its tenth class reunion back in Arkansas, and I really felt like I was supposed to be there. Sharon couldn't make it because she was in her last month of pregnancy with our second child. I would have to fly alone. I decided to go on a Friday afternoon and come back Saturday afternoon because I had to preach on Sunday morning. I went on Saturday to the reunion, but the opportunity to speak did not happen. I felt disappointed as I got into the plane to return to Tulsa. Halfway back, the spirit of the Lord spoke to me, telling me to turn around and go to the evening banquet. I did, and the opportunity to tell my testimony opened up, and then I prayed.

Early Sunday morning, as I took off from the airport in the small plane, the weather looked stormy. After flying a few miles, I found myself in the middle of a horrendous thunder storm. Before I knew it, the airplane was spiraling out of control. When you're in a situation like that, your *senses* will tell you that you're going in one direction, but the reality is that you're going in a completely different direction. You must look at and trust the instruments in the plane to tell you what direction you're headed. At the time, I was out of control and going down at a fast speed. My mind was spinning, and I couldn't think clearly at that point. But somehow deep inside of me, faith rose up. I screamed at the top of my lungs, "YOU'RE GOING TO MAKE IT! YOU'RE GOING TO MAKE IT!" It was a statement of faith to myself because, in the natural, everything was going opposite of that statement.

When I screamed that out, however, it jarred me to remember to look at the instruments, to trust the instruments, and to read the instruments. I somehow knew at that point to pull up on the lever to stabilize the plane. When I began to slowly pull up on it, I started leveling off and was able to pull myself out of that spiraling dive. I pulled the power back and flew a bumpy up and down ride back to Tulsa. I made it for the first church service that morning. Later I learned that my mom had been praying during the entire trip. The spirit of God had alerted her. In the midst of chaos and confusion, the shield of faith can bring you through what looks like certain defeat. Hold up your shield and keep on going. Begin to say, "I walk by faith and not by sight" (see 2 Cor. 5:7) and, "This is the victory that I have to overcome in this world, my faith" (see 1 John 5:4).

HELMET OF SALVATION

A helmet is critical to a soldier. It guards the command center for the whole body. The brain, with its intricate, vulnerable parts, gives orders to each cell of the body to perform simple and complex tasks. It is "in charge," so to speak, so it must be heavily guarded. The *helmet of salvation* works in a similar way. It guards your thought processes and keeps your mind sane in the midst of the battle that you may be facing. When the bullets of fear and terror are flying, salvation protects your mind. You are able to stand strong and without intimidation in spite of what is happening around you because your mind is guarded. Begin to say, "I have the mind of Christ" (see 1 Cor. 2:16). "The weapons of [my] warfare are not physical (weapons of flesh and blood) but they are mighty before God for the overthrow and destruction of strongholds" (2 Cor. 10:4 AMP). "I cast down imaginations and every high thing that exalts itself against the knowledge of God, bringing every thought into captivity to the obedience of Christ" (2 Cor. 10:5 KJV).

Don't leave the house without your helmet. It's there to safeguard you in times of distress and disillusionment, bringing you back to the reality of the One who is fighting on your behalf.

SWORD OF THE SPIRIT

Up until now, we've been going through the list of weapons that will help defend you in the battle. All are necessary, and none is greater than the other. These will keep you safe, but you have to have an offensive weapon to win in this battle. You'll notice that every weapon that is mentioned has to do with the Word of God. Without the Word, we are powerless. But just as armor has various parts (helmet, breastplate, boots), so the Word of God functions in different ways as part of your armor. The *Sword of the Spirit* is God's Word spoken from your mouth to resist and overcome the work of the enemy (see Ephesians 6:17).

One particular story of this type of stand on the Word of God in our lives happened early on in our ministry. While we were youth pastors, we began ministering to a young man named Greg. The main reason Greg came to our youth group was to find girls. He was not interested in the things of God. He would show up sometimes dazed and drunk. We always watched him because of our lack of trust in him. We weren't sure what to do with him. We tried to minister to him but felt like we weren't getting through at all. His mother would come to pick him up at the end of the service, and she could clearly see the state of mind he was in. Invariably, however, she'd always smile and say to me, "Isn't Greg just doing wonderful? Isn't he growing in the things of God?" I was thinking to myself, *Do you not see and smell that he's drunk?* I thought that she must be a little strange to not to at least admit that he was in a drunken state, but we respected her and kept our mouths shut and just let her talk. This went on for some time with no apparent change in Greg's life.

His mother knew something at that time that we hadn't learned. She had been speaking the Word of God over Greg in her prayer time, going after the Word that says that he is delivered and set free. She was standing on the truth of Proverbs 11:21, "The seed of the righteous shall be delivered" (KJV) and Isaiah 49:25, "I will contend with him who contends with you, and I will save your children." She was declaring the Word over Greg, and she saw him from that angle. It was her Sword of the Spirit—cutting off the enemy's lies ahead of the victory.

One night, the youth group got together at someone's house for a fellowship time. We were serving pop and pizza and had a mixed group of girls and guys there. Greg showed up for the free meal that night and was sitting in a chair by the door. We had a short time of worship, and the guy next to Greg asked for prayer. When everyone turned to pray for that guy, Greg had nowhere to go. He had to stay put because he was surrounded. During that prayer time, the Spirit of God told me to lay my hand on Greg's knee. When I did, Greg began to feel the presence of God. That night he was saved, he filled with the Holy Spirit, with the evidence of speaking in other tongues, and he was called to go to Bible school and eventually into the ministry. That was the beginning of Greg's turn around. His mother had already used the Sword of the Spirit to rout out the enemy, so she was thrilled to see how God had touched him that night. Greg did go to Bible school that year and after graduation he went into full-time ministry. Greg has been serving the Lord for more than thirty years now, all as a result of a mother who aggressively fought with the Sword of the Spirit for his soul and never gave up.

PRAYING IN THE SPIRIT

When Ephesians 6:18 talks about the last part of the armor—praying always in the Spirit—it is interesting to note that this includes not only praying for yourself but also for all of the saints. Praying in the spirit, or praying in tongues, releases great power. First Corinthians 14:14 says, "For if I pray in a tongue, my spirit prays, but my understanding is unfruitful." This is the essence of the power of praying in tongues. Your mind can go only so far to discern what is happening in a situation. Your five senses interpret to your mind what may be wrong, but they cannot always discern the source or root. Sometimes when I pray in tongues, thoughts of direction or discernment come to my mind that had not even crossed my thoughts up to that point. First Corinthians 14:15 goes on to say, "What is the conclusion then? I will pray with the spirit, and I will also pray with the understanding. I will sing with the spirit, and I will also sing with the understanding." After I pray in tongues, then I pray out in English what I perceive the Spirit of God has just revealed to me about the situation.

Also referred to as our "heavenly language," it is able to bypass not only our minds but also the devil's realm. Speaking in tongues is direct communication with the Spirit of God. It's biblical and powerful. Romans 8:26 tells us that we may not know what to pray, so the Spirit aids us to effectively pray into situations. No wonder this particular piece of weaponry has been under so much attack—not only from the world but also from the Church. Every New Testament writer spoke in tongues. It was a part of those involved in the early Church throughout the book of Acts. Sharon and I are thankful for the ability to pray both in tongues and in our understanding. God has delivered our lives over and over again as we've prayed in the Spirit and as we've listened to His thoughts that came to us afterward. It is a miraculous work of God's grace.

THE BLOOD

As mentioned earlier, the armor of Ephesians chapter 6 revolves around the power of the Word of God. Continuing on in our arsenal of weapons, we find the precious *blood of Jesus.* There is power in the blood. At the Last Supper, during the Passover meal, as the disciples drank from the cup, Jesus said, "This is My blood of the new covenant, which is shed for many..." (Matt. 26:28). The cup of juice was not changed into His blood when He said that, nor is it somehow changed into blood as we celebrate the act of communion. No, as we take Him as our Lord and Savior, we take all of Him. Just like, in the natural, blood permeates every aspect of a cell, so in the Spirit, calling on His blood fills us with His presence and reminds us of the power of His sacrifice. The spiritual effect is that the blood of Jesus cleanses us of sin.

Leviticus 17:11 and many other Scriptures tell us that the life is in the blood. We are redeemed by the blood of the Lamb of God. That means that His blood paid for us. Our sin had to be atoned for, and His sacrifice, as an innocent lamb going to the slaughter, provides for our redemption. Just as the blood of the sacrificed animals was poured on the mercy seat in the Holy of Holies in the Tabernacle, His blood was poured on the mercy seat in Heaven for us. There is spiritual significance for every instruction that God gave to the Israelites. They were told to put the blood of a lamb on the doorpost so that the angel of death would pass over their homes (see Exod. 12:13). As they applied the blood on the top and sides of the door, it became a symbol of the blood of Jesus Christ that dripped from the top and the sides of the cross where He was crucified. Jesus, the only begotten Son of God, the Lamb of God without sin, was offered up to cleanse the sins of all who would believe in Him. Medical science says that the blood of a person comes from the father. Jesus, born of a virgin, shed the blood of His Father, God, in order to have pure, sinless blood that could cleanse our sins. With this understanding of the power of the blood of the risen Savior, we can say over ourselves, "We're covered by the blood of the Lamb" to signify that the "blood line" has been drawn and that the avenger cannot attack. It is a powerful, effective tool that we've been given.

THE NAME

Another weapon to take into daily battle is the name of Jesus. Miracles and the casting out of demons were regular occurrences while Jesus walked on the earth. People recognized that this man had power over the unseen world. Jesus gave authority to those following Him through His name (see Luke 10:17-20). When Jesus rose from the dead and appeared to the disciples, He gave them power over satan through the use of His name (see Mark 16:15-20; Matt. 28:18-20). This applied to all of the generations that followed who would believe in Him as well. His name still has that same power. Heaven and hell tremble at the name of Jesus. The spirit of antichrist is familiar with its power, too. That's why you'll see that, although prayer has been taken out of school by law, occasionally they'll allow someone to pray at a public event with the stipulation that they don't use the name of Jesus. You can use the name of God all day long, but when you start saying, "In Jesus' name," the media and lawmakers throw a fit. You've just come up against a spirit of antichrist when you face that.

I was asked to say a prayer at a city banquet years ago, and before I got up to pray, someone took me aside and said, "Oh, I forgot to tell you, don't pray in the name of Jesus. There are people from different religions and sects here, and we don't want to offend them." I looked at the guy and just told him, "It's too late. You've asked me to pray, and I pray in the name of Jesus, and that's what I'm going to do." I'm not going to deny Jesus when I have the opportunity to speak the power of His name in a setting like that! When facing situations beyond your natural ability, call on the name of Jesus. If you don't know how else to pray, just begin to say His name: "Jesus. Jesus. Jesus. Jesus." It will still your fears and calm your nerves. It will cause your mind to think more clearly and peaceably. Use the name in the battle.

SUBMIT TO GOD

The deliverance of the Jewish people from the hand of wicked Haman, as recorded in the Book of Esther, took place in Persia, which is now modern day Iran. The feast of Purim is still celebrated among Jewish people to commemorate their liberation. What looked like sure defeat for the Jews turned overnight into their victory. Even though it is God's will for us to be delivered from evil, Esther had to learn that she had to act on the commands of God in order to see it happen. In her case, she had to *submit to God's will*, regardless of her own feelings. When she surrendered her life and stepped before the king of Persia, she saved her people.

You can only have God's authority when you are under His authority. The Roman centurion who wanted Jesus to heal his servant understood that Jesus had authority over sickness. As recorded in Matthew 8:9, he said to Jesus, "For I also am a man under authority, having soldiers under me. And I say to this one, 'Go,' and he goes; and to another, 'Come,' and he comes; and to my servant, 'Do this,' and he does it." The man recognized that Jesus was under God's authority and was totally submitted and obedient to His Father God. The centurion knew that God would back anything that Jesus said, just like the Roman government backed any words he commanded to his soldiers and his servants. James 4:7 tells us to "submit to God." Before resisting the devil, make sure you are doing what God has told you to do. Obedience to His commands is a prerequisite to walking in dominion. If you live in an independent, rebellious attitude toward authority figures, you will not have spiritual authority. You can yell and scream and demand, but satan knows that you are walking in line with him, and he knows that you have no authority over him. Humble yourself before God and live in submission to the authorities that He has placed around your life as you submit to Him.

RESIST THE DEVIL AND HE WILL FLEE

Resist means "to stand firm against." Refuse the lies of the enemy with all of your being. Jesus left us an example on how to resist the devil. When Jesus was tempted by the devil after His time of fasting, He responded all three times with "It is written..." and then quoted the Word of God to negate the enemy's suggestions (see Matt. 4:4,7,10). Say the Scripture *out loud* against evil thoughts and temptations. It's not enough just to *think* of the Scripture to combat the thoughts and imaginations. Thinking or meditating on the Scripture leads into speaking it, but it definitely must be spoken out. When you're in a terrifying situation, you must take hold of your mind. Instead of speaking what appears to *look* like the inevitable, speak what the Word of God says and see God's deliverance.

THE POWER OF PRAISE

The final area of your weaponry is the power of *praise.* King Jehoshaphat found out what happens when praise is released against the enemy. He heard that two armies were set up to attack the Israelites. The prophet Jahaziel told the people not to fear because they would not even have to fight as they went up against the enemy, for the Lord was with them, and the battle was the Lord's. Jehoshaphat appointed singers to go out before the army of Israel, singing, "Praise the Lord; for His mercy endures forever." The results of their praises were amazing: "Now when they began to sing and to praise, the Lord set ambushes against the people of Ammon, Moab, and Mount Seir, who had come against Judah; and they were defeated" (2 Chron. 20:22).

Those ambushes were angels who came on the scene in response to the praise. They fought the enemy for the Israelites, and then the enemy turned against themselves. Praise in the midst of the storm—in spite of what is happening around you—will put the enemy in confusion. He doesn't understand how you can praise God when all that you're facing is one negative report after another. You are releasing power into the atmosphere through your praise. However you can do it—sing, hum, whisper, and shout the praises of God! In whatever circumstance you find yourself, you have more than enough artillery to face the battle. Put on the armor and be strong in the power of the Lord! His Spirit will show you which weapons to use at the appropriate time, and you will find the deliverance that God has planned for you.

ENDNOTES

1. *The Word: The Bible from 26 Translations* (Moss Point, MS: Mathis Publishers, Inc., 1993).
2. Noah Webster, *American Dictionary of the English Language*, 1828 ed., s.v.v. "Shoe," "Shod."

Chapter 16

NO FEAR SCRIPTURES

In this chapter, I have included Scriptures that have been personalized for you to speak over yourself. If you find yourself in a situation that seems to be overwhelming or that could cause you to panic, the truth of these words will set you free as you meditate on them and speak them out. You're an overcomer in this land!

FEAR NOT

In righteousness I shall be established. I shall be far from oppression, for I shall not fear; and from terror, for it shall not come near me. Indeed they shall surely assemble, but not because of the Lord. Whoever assembles against me shall fall for my sake (see Isaiah 54:14-15).

No man shall be able to stand before me all the days of my life; as God was with Moses, so He will be with me. He will not leave me nor forsake me. I will be strong and of good courage... (see Joshua 1:5-6).

I will not fear or be dismayed...for the Lord is with me (see 2 Chronicles 20:17).

I will not be afraid of sudden terror, nor of trouble from the wicked when it comes; for the Lord will be my confidence, and will keep my foot from being caught (see Proverbs 3:25-26).

I fear not, for God is with me; I am not dismayed, for He is my God. He will strengthen me, yes, He will help me, He will uphold me with His righteous right hand. Behold, all those who were incensed against me shall be ashamed and disgraced; they shall be as nothing, and those who strive with me shall perish. I shall seek them and not find them—those who contended with me. Those who war against me shall be as nothing, as a non-existent thing. For the Lord my God will hold my right hand, saying to me, "Fear not, I will help you" (see Isaiah 41:10-13).

I do not fear, for it is my Father's good pleasure to give me the Kingdom (see Luke 12:32).

God is for me, who can be against me? (See Romans 8:31.)

Christ has redeemed me from the curse of the law, having become a curse for me (for it is written, "Cursed is everyone who hangs on a tree") (see Galatians 3:13).

For God has not given me a spirit of fear, but of power and of love and of a sound mind (see 2 Timothy 1:7).

The Lord [God] Himself has said, "I will not in any way fail you nor give you up nor leave you without support. [I will] not, [I will] not, [I will] not in any degree leave you helpless nor forsake nor let [you] down (relax My hold on you)! [Assuredly not!]." So we take comfort and are encouraged and confidently and boldly say, "The Lord is my Helper; I will not be seized with alarm [I will not fear or dread or be terrified]. What can man do to me?" (See Hebrews 13:5-6 AMP.)

There is no fear in love; but perfect love casts out fear (see 1 John 4:18).

TRAVELING SAFETY

Has God not commanded me? Be strong and of good courage; do not be afraid, nor be dismayed, for the Lord my God is with me wherever I go (see Joshua 1:9).

The Lord shall preserve my going out and my coming in from this time forth, and even forevermore (see Psalm 121:8).

SAFETY FROM ENEMIES

No weapon formed against me shall prosper, and every tongue which rises against me in judgment I shall condemn (see Isaiah 54:17).

The Lord will cause my enemies who rise against me to be defeated before my face; they shall come out against me one way and flee before me seven ways (see Deuteronomy 28:7).

The Lord is my light and my salvation; whom shall I fear? The Lord is the strength of my life; of whom shall I be afraid? (See Psalm 27:1.)

Let those be put to shame and brought to dishonor who seek after my life; let those be turned back and brought to confusion who plot my hurt (see Psalm 35:4).

In God I have put my trust; I will not fear. What can flesh do to me? (See Psalm 56:4.)

I dwell in the secret place of the Most High and shall abide under the shadow of the Almighty. I will say of the Lord, "He is my refuge and my fortress; my God, in Him I will trust." Surely He shall deliver me from the snare of the fowler and from the perilous pestilence. He shall cover me with His feathers, and under His wings I shall take refuge; His truth shall be my shield and buckler. I shall not be afraid of the terror by night, nor of the arrow that flies by day, nor of the pestilence that walks in darkness, nor of the destruction that lays waste at noonday. A thousand may fall at my side, and ten thousand at my right hand; but it shall not come near me. Only with my eyes shall I look, and see the reward of the wicked. Because I have made the Lord, who is my refuge, even the Most High, my dwelling place, No evil shall befall me, nor shall any plague come near my dwelling; for He shall give His angels charge over me, to keep me in all my ways. In their hands they shall bear me up, lest I dash my foot against a stone. I shall tread upon the lion and the cobra, the young lion and the serpent I shall trample underfoot. Because I have set my love upon Him, therefore He will deliver me; He will set me on high, because I have known His name. I shall call upon Him, and He will answer me; He will be with me in trouble; He will deliver me and honor me. With long life He will satisfy me, and show me His salvation" (see Psalm 91).

The Lord is on my side; I will not fear. What can man do to me? (See Psalm 118:6.)

And He gives me eternal life, and I shall never perish; neither shall anyone snatch me out of His hand. His Father, who has given me to Him, is greater than all; and no one is able to snatch me out of His Father's hand (see John 10:28-29).

If God is for me, who can be against me? (See Romans 8:31.)

What persecutions I endured. And out of them all the Lord delivered me (see 2 Timothy 3:11).

I am strong in the Lord and in the power of His might. I put on the whole armor of God, that I may be able to stand against the wiles of the devil. For I do not wrestle against flesh and blood, but against principalities, against powers, against the rulers of the darkness of this age, against spiritual hosts of wickedness in the heavenly places. Therefore I take up the whole armor of God, that I may be able to withstand in the evil day, and having done all, to stand. I stand therefore, having girded my waist with truth, having put on the breastplate of right-eousness, and having shod my feet with the preparation of the gospel of peace; above all, I take the shield of faith with which I will be able to quench all the fiery darts of the wicked one. And I take the helmet of salvation, and the sword of the Spirit, which is the word of God; pray-ing always with all prayer and supplication in the Spirit, being watchful to this end with all perseverance and supplication for all the saints (see Ephesians 6:10-18).

I keep myself, and the wicked one does not touch me (see 1 John 5:18).

SAFETY FOR YOUR CHILDREN

Here am I and the children whom the Lord has given me! We are for signs and for wonders... (Isaiah 8:18).

God will contend with those who contend with me, and He will save my children (see Isaiah 49:25).

All my children shall be taught by the Lord, and great shall be the peace of my children (see Isaiah 54:13).

For He has strengthened the bars of my gates; He has blessed my children within me (see Psalm 147:13).

In the fear of the Lord there is strong confidence, and my children will have a place of refuge (see Proverbs 14:26).

ANXIOUS THOUGHTS

He will keep me in perfect peace, as my mind is stayed on Him, because I trust in Him (see Isaiah 26:3).

Say to those who are fearful-hearted, "Be strong, do not fear! Behold, your God will come with vengeance, with the recompense of God; He will come and save you" (Isaiah 35:4).

In righteousness I shall be established; I shall be far from oppression, for I shall not fear; and from terror, for it shall not come near me (see Isaiah 54:14).

Therefore I submit to God. I resist the devil, and he will flee from me (see James 4:7).

I cast all my care upon Him, for He cares for me (see 1 Peter 5:7).

HEALING AND HEALTH

For He is the Lord who heals me (see Exodus 15:26).

He sent His Word to heal me and to deliver me from all destruction (see Psalm 107:20).

But Jesus was wounded for my transgressions, He was bruised for my iniquities; the chastisement for my peace was upon Him, and by His stripes I am healed (see Isaiah 53:5).

I shall live and not die to declare the wonderful works of the Lord (see Psalm 118:17).

For God will restore health to me and heal me of my wounds (see Jeremiah 30:17).

Bless the Lord, O my soul, and forget not all his benefits. Who forgives all my iniquities; who heals all my diseases; who redeems my life from destruction; who crowns me with loving kindness and tender mercies (see Psalm 103:2-4).

And Jesus went about all Galilee, teaching in their synagogues, preaching the gospel of the kingdom, and healing all kinds of sickness and all kinds of disease among the people (Matthew 4:23).

Jesus took our infirmities and bore our sicknesses (see Matthew 8:17).

And Jesus said to him, "I will come and heal him" (Matthew 8:7).

But when Jesus knew it, He withdrew from there. And great multitudes followed Him, and He healed them all (Matthew 12:15).

And the whole multitude sought to touch Him, for power went out from Him and healed them all (Luke 6:19).

God anointed Jesus of Nazareth with the Holy Ghost and with power, who went about doing good and healing all that were oppressed of the devil, for God was with him (Acts 10:38).

[Jesus] bore our sins in His own body on the tree, that we, having died to sins, might live for righteousness—by whose stripes you were healed (1 Peter 2:24).

Christ has redeemed me from the curse of the law by being made a curse for me (for it is written, "Cursed is every man that hangs on a tree"), so that the blessing of Abraham might come on the Gentiles through Jesus

Christ, that we might receive the promise of the Holy Spirit through faith (see Galatians 3:13-14).

I pray that I may prosper in all things and be in health, just as my soul prospers (see 3 John 2).

I am redeemed out of the hand of the enemy. For the Lord is good and His mercy endures forever (see Psalm 107:1-2).

NATURAL DISASTERS (STORMS, HURRICANES, TSUNAMIS)

God is my refuge and strength, a very present help in trouble. Therefore I will not fear, even though the earth be removed, and though the mountains be carried into the midst of the sea (see Psalm 46:1-2).

The Lord says, "Fear not, for I have redeemed you; I have called you by your name; you are Mine. When you pass through the waters, I will be with you; and through the rivers, they shall not overflow you. When you walk through the fire, you shall not be burned, nor shall the flame scorch you" (see Isaiah 43:1-2).

I fear no evil for you are with me. Your rod (Your Word) and Your staff (Your Spirit)–they comfort me (see Psalm 23:4).

You are the Lord my God in the midst of me, mighty to save and mighty to deliver my life (see Zephaniah 3:17).

No temptation has overtaken me except such as is common to man; but God is faithful, He will not allow me to be tempted beyond what I am able, but with the temptation will also make the way of escape, that I may be able to bear it (see 1 Corinthians 10:13).

PERSONAL PRAYER OF COMMITMENT

Father, I want to hear the Spirit's leading every day of my life so that I can avoid every trap and plan of the enemy. I confess my sins to You and ask You to cleanse me with the blood that Jesus shed for me. I receive forgiveness of my sins and the gift of righteousness by faith. Fill me with the power of Your Holy Spirit.

Lord, thank You for Your presence with me always and forever. I'll never be alone another day of my life. Lord, I determine to walk in mature love and forgiveness in all situations so that no door of calamity is open in my life. I declare that You are my refuge, my fortress, and my high tower, and that You deliver me from evil. I choose to be led by Your Holy Spirit.

Thank You that no evil shall befall me and that no plague shall come near my dwelling. You give me long life, You hear me when I pray, and You deliver me and set me on high.

Lord, thank You for the promise of Your Word coming alive in my heart and the spirit of faith rising to receive Your truth, in Jesus' name.

_____   _____
Signature   Date

Revelation ch 2

NOTES

OTHER BOOKS BY THE AUTHOR INCLUDE:

101 Days of Absolute Victory
The Power of Your Words
Faith Power
Breaking the Chains of Bondage
Led By the Spirit
Principles of Prayer
Killing the Giant of Ministry Debt
Heaven Is On Its Feet
Building Stronger Marriages and Families
The Demonstration of the Gospel
Living in God's Abundance

MINIBOOKS INCLUDE:

Be On Fire for the Lord
Be Strong in the Lord
Breakfast of Champions
Building Quality Relationships
Death is Not the End
Delivered From Evil
Diligence Produces Results
Don't Be Offended
Escaping Fatal Attractions
Faith With Corresponding Actions
Finding Your Purpose
Getting Over the Moody Blues
God is Not Mad at You
God's Protecting Angels
God's Word for You: "Fear Not"

Healing, Help and Hope
How to Know God's Will
How to Overcome a Life Threatening Illness
How to Turn Your Scars Into Stars
It's Time to Drive Out Your Enemies
Juggling Your Priorities
Mercy and Grace
Overcoming Strife
Overcoming the Storms of Life
Possessing God's Promises
Possibility Living
Praise and Thanksgiving
Promises to Believe for Your Children
Recovering What the Devil Has Stolen
Renewing Your Mind
Seven Keys to Family Power
Soaring with Eagles
Taking Control of Your Thoughts
The Goal
The Name of Jesus
This New Life
Warnings of God
What is the Fear of the Lord?
What to Do When You Don't Know What to Do
You are Valuable
You Can Start Over
You Have a Destiny
You Will Increase

FOR OTHER BOOKS AND MINIBOOKS BY THE AUTHOR, CONTACT:

Website: www.victory.com
Telephone: 918-491-7700
Address: Victory Christian Center
7700 South Lewis Avenue
Tulsa, OK 74136-7700

Prayer

When Daniel Pray
God shut the mouth of
the lion

Prayer would Be a way
of life   Psalm 125

Prayer Bring Friendship
with God. Psalm 25
it allowed doing the Right
thing prayer a part of your
Foundation.
Prayer allowed everything

G m BA is not

G mA 0800092 892
            927892
    G mÉ   Devinah Singer

Take a Risk for God. A Lots Refuse
to Burried the past with nothing Back
whereas you trust God Re reward
            the weight for

Victory Christian Center
Saturdays — 5pm
Sundays — 9, 11am & 6pm
Wednesdays — 7pm

All services held in the Worship Center (7700 S. Lewis Ave., Tulsa, OK)
Nursery/Children's Church available at all services

24/7 Youth: Sundays 6pm & Wednesdays 7pm
3D (ages 18-28): Tuesdays 8pm
Singles (29+): Fridays 7pm

24/7 Bldg. (81st & Delaware)

918-491-7700
victory.com

Additional copies of this book and other
book titles from Destiny Image are
available at your local bookstore.

Call toll-free: 1-800-722-6774.

Send a request for a catalog to:

Destiny Image® Publishers, Inc.
P.O. Box 310
Shippensburg, PA 17257-0310

*"Speaking to the Purposes of God for This
Generation and for the Generations to Come."*

**For a complete list of our titles,
visit us at www.destinyimage.com.**

yesterday Battle do not
measure today Victory